JOSEPH - THE DREAMER

JOSEPH
The Dreamer

"I can't do it...but God can!"

Tom Glover

Christian Year Publications

ISBN-13: 978 1 872734 36 1

Typeset by John Ritchie Ltd., Kilmarnock
Printed by Bell & Bain Ltd., Glasgow

DEDICATION:

To Dorothy, my wife, who has been a great source of
encouragement and support throughout
many years in God's service.

A WORD OF APPRECIATION:

I am indebted to Nick Dimeo and also Edwin Taylor for their willingness in proof reading this manuscript.

My grateful thanks also to my family, who have always been a continual source of encouragement.

Foreword

My first meeting with Tom around twelve years ago launched a friendship which involved French horn playing in Vienna, serious illness and the sharing of some very special spiritual experiences. Tom gave me a copy of an earlier incarnation of the present 'Joseph' to feed a retreat that I went on at a time when the next stage of my own journey was very unclear. I texted Tom to say that it was a privilege to have been able to use the material. I am so glad that it is now in book form, for it will allow others to share in the blessings and challenges that come through the unfolding of the 'Joseph story'.

God is graciously steering us for his own purposes; in his way and time; a time that brings us to where he wants us to be when he needs us. Tom brings out the following subject matter of Joseph's journey in a wonderful manner.

- From the damage of family favouritism to family rejection and abandonment ...
- From abject slavery to ennoblement and power ...
- From hurt and hatred to the grace of forgiveness and renewal ...
- From obscurity in Canaan to the highly exalted position of Prime Minister in Egypt ...

Tom introduces us to the drama and the theology of the story in a very exciting manner. Join Tom: be excited and inspired.

Dr John Sharp

A word from the author

Joseph's life has all the elements of a truly great story: ambition - youth - beauty - temptation - suffering - sorrow - jealousy - hatred - forgiveness - patience and the sovereignty of God. We have before us one of the best known and most loved Bible characters in all of the Old Testament; he is also the subject of many books and songs.

It is difficult to follow God's plan for Joseph and his family without seeing 'God at work'; moulding and shaping him until he is wonderfully transformed. From his early days as a young immature teenager in Canaan; God was able, through a series of devastating circumstances, to exalt Joseph higher than he could ever have dreamed. Not only shall we see how God changed Joseph and his family, but also, how he used him as an instrument of God's glory in a dark pagan world at that time. Throughout Joseph's life, we read: *The Lord was with Joseph.*

Those who read and meditate on the life of Joseph will be greatly enriched and discover that it is not simply an ancient story, but relevant for today. There are many encouragements and lessons to be learned that will help us to live for Christ more deeply and effectively.

As we trace the purpose of God for Joseph and his family, we discover that the pathway was strewn with heartache, sorrow, injustice and uncertainty - yet just at the right time, God drew all the strands together and did something wonderful. Who could have believed when Joseph was thrust into a pit what the final outcome would eventually be! The

Joseph

'Joseph story' will encourage us to keep trusting and believing, even when the way ahead may seem obscure. Romans 8:28, *And we know that for those who love God all things work together for good....*

Contents

CHAPTER 1

Joseph's background and early life

Genesis 37:1-2

> *Jacob lived in the land of his father's sojournings, in the land of Canaan. 2 These are the generations of Jacob. Joseph, being seventeen years old, was pasturing the flock with his brothers. He was a boy with the sons of Bilhah and Zilpah, his father's wives. And Joseph brought a bad report of them to their father.*

Joseph is one of the better known and much loved Old Testament Bible characters. His story has captured the hearts and minds of many who have thoughtfully pored over the biblical account of his life; often producing a sanctifying influence and life-changing experience. There are lessons for all ages and encouragement for most situations in life. At times it is enthralling and emotionally stirring.

From the outset there are lessons for fathers who are tempted to spoil their children or even make one a favourite. There are warnings for those who are young and think they have arrived before they have even started out. The meaning of total forgiveness finds expression in the relationship between Joseph and his brothers in a quite unparalleled way outwith the message of the Cross. From beginning to end, the sovereign purpose of God is a major theme. Joseph discovered, even in his most difficult times, that the Lord was with him and that God's purpose was still at the heart of all that was happening.

The life of Joseph has all the elements of a great story; it is full of intrigue and suspense. Ambition, temptation, suffering, sorrow, jealously, hatred, forgiveness and the sovereignty of God are all in evidence. Studying the story of Joseph will lead us to a deeper understanding of both ourselves and of God. It will help us to learn more about how God prepares someone to serve him. The timescale involved, the patience required and the need for personal growth and maturity are all part of the scenario. Dr M Lloyd-Jones once said: 'the worst thing that can happen to a man is to succeed before he is ready.' When Joseph was young he thought he was ready, but he wasn't! The time would come, however, when he would be ready. That's what the story of Joseph is all about! Most of us don't like to be told we need further preparation, Joseph was no different.

Yet before the spoiled young man of seventeen years became Prime Minister, it would involve thirteen years of preparation. During that time Joseph would not have understood the journey God was allowing him to travel; he could not possibly have dreamt where God's purpose would lead him. A shepherd boy to a Prime Minister!

It is of enormous importance and a great encouragement to remember that all God's dealings with Israel, their birth as a nation, slavery, deliverance, triumph and glory began with Joseph and the eventual family move to Egypt (not forgetting those who preceded; Abraham and Isaac). Joseph was the continuing link in the promise made to Abraham many years before regarding the birth of a nation and a spiritual offspring too great to number. The Joseph story teaches us much about the importance of just one person and their obedience to the purpose of God, and also the effect and influence it can have on the lives of others.

Not too much is known about Joseph's early life, however, there are some things worth mentioning. Joseph was about five or six years old when they moved from Haran to Canaan. He would have had many childhood memories; good and not so good. Perhaps he would remember his father stealing livestock from his Uncle Laban or even the time his father Jacob returned home with a limp, radiant, following his encounter with God. Sadly, he may also have remembered his brothers killing many people because his sister had been defiled. It may also be that he remembered family worship at Bethel where his father instructed all the family to get rid of all foreign gods and to purify themselves. He would remember too how heartbroken his father was when his mother Rachel died (Jacob's best loved wife). No doubt he could also recall the jealousy and bitterness between his father's wives and the rivalry among his older brothers. He knew his father had been a cheat, deceiver and schemer; yet he also saw how God had changed him.

Joseph had not led a sheltered life, but had been exposed to all that happened around him. His memories would surely play their part in his personal development as the Spirit of God directed his life. God would take him from rags to riches, from slavehood to a position of authority and from the pit to Prime Minister.

Verse 2 introduces us to Joseph and tells us what he was doing at that time. We are told that he was seventeen and was tending the flocks with his brothers. It's interesting to note that both Moses and David were doing the same thing when God laid his hand upon them and redirected their lives in a quite remarkable way; ultimately exalting them to positions of authority and power - but not before they were ready! Joseph was doing a very ordinary, everyday job, yet he was doing it faithfully. With Moses and David in mind, and now Joseph, it would seem that there is some special quality related to shepherding that prepares a person for leading people. Certainly the prophet Isaiah reminds us that both people and sheep have the tendency for straying: *We all like sheep, have gone astray, each of us has turned to his own way* .... (Isaiah 53:6).

Ahead of Joseph lay thirteen years of preparation. Events and situations lay ahead that he would not have chosen. With one rare exception (Genesis 40:14) he submitted to them without complaint or any obvious resistance. At times this must have been horrendously difficult for him; he must have wondered where his God was and why he was dealt with so undeservingly. Facing difficult situations are hard enough to deal with even when you know the underlying reasons, but Joseph didn't! Perhaps he questioned God many times! We'll never know. Scripture provides no record of this, yet it would seem the natural thing to do.

Joseph's first actions are not commendable. Verse 2: *And Joseph brought a bad report of them to their father.* Joseph's brothers were a mixed bunch; they shared four different mothers - Leah, Rachel, Bilhah and Zilpah. This led to jealousy and rivalry among them; they were prone to squabble among themselves. On the face of it, Joseph was a 'tell-tale'. What he said may have been true, but this was no excuse. Why did he bring a bad report about his brothers? Was he jealous of them, or perhaps trying to exalt himself? It might even have been that he thought the information he was providing was helpful to his father, we don't know. Exactly how Jacob responded to Joseph's gossip is uncertain. However, since Joseph was his favourite son we can be sure that he listened to what he had to say. Verse 2 reminds us that he was tending the flocks *with his brothers.* Because of this, he would have seen and heard all that was going on.

Bringing down others is often a form of self exaltation; this may have been Joseph's motive. Either way, it is not a healthy introduction to Joseph's life and presents us with a helpful challenge if ever tempted to gossip or tell tales. If we have nothing to say that will encourage, build up or help, then the wise option is usually that of silence. In Proverbs 26:20 we read: *Without wood a fire goes out; without gossip a quarrel dies down ...* and in 16:28: *A gossip separates close friends.* As we journey through the Joseph story we will find that he learned not to exalt or vindicate himself, but at this early stage he is young, eager and immature. Although there was evidence of his early gifts, he did not have the maturity to use them wisely.

It would be so easy to say no more about this bad report that Joseph brought to his father, yet it is significant in that it finds its place in Holy Scripture, in particular, right at the beginning of the story. Why not start with nice things about Joseph? Why not pay a few compliments about his character, diligence or faithfulness? Why not tell us about how skilled he was at shepherding, or how wonderful a son he was to his father Jacob? The likelihood is that this bad report (and there may have been others) was the catalyst for what was about to follow. No doubt his brothers would hear about Joseph's report; his father may even have acted on what he had told him. His brothers were primed, therefore, to deal with him at the first opportunity, and that was about to happen. Joseph's tales would only have brought greater distance between him and his brothers.

Here then, we find a seeming flaw in Joseph's character in his tender years. In a sense this is encouraging, and reminds us that we don't have to be perfect for God to use us. Even with his weaknesses and faults, God still had a noble and mighty purpose for his life. He was a young man in the making whom God would use; but not yet - he was not ready! For sure he would make his mistakes. Don't we all? Yet, in and through them, God was moulding and shaping him for a future occasion when he would be in a position of exalted greatness, and be a vital link in the development of Israel as a nation.

Throughout Joseph's ups and downs, including in the pit, Potiphar's house and prison, we discover that the 'Lord was with him'. God's hand was upon him during his darkest moments and deepest despair. The Lord was with Joseph, even when he was unaware of it. He learned to trust not because his circumstances were favourable but because 'God was faithful' and he believed in his purpose. No greater compliment could be paid to anyone than 'the Lord is with them'. Clearly the stamp of God's approval was on his life. It is most encouraging to note that although Joseph was not the finished article and that the Lord had a lot of sorting out to do in his life, he was still firmly in the hand of the Lord. It is evident that Joseph yielded to the sanctifying work of the Spirit, which meant that he was in tune with God and submitted to the Spirit's direction.

In Psalm 105:17-22 we have a wonderful summary of God's dealing with Joseph. He was God's chosen instrument and played an extraordinary part, both in the formation of Israel as a nation and in the greater purpose of God for the spiritual wellbeing of mankind. Verse 17 reads: *and he sent a man before them - Joseph, sold as a slave.* At the moment Joseph is introduced as a tell-tale, yet how glorious it is to find these words: *and he sent a man before them.* How wonderful is the purpose of God! God's plan for Joseph and his family was so far reaching that it impacts our lives today. Who can tell what God has in mind for those who honour him?

CHAPTER 2

The danger of favouritism

Genesis 37:3-11

3 Now Israel loved Joseph more than any other of his sons, because he was the son of his old age. And he made him a robe of many colours. 4 But when his brothers saw that their father loved him more than all his brothers, they hated him and could not speak peacefully to him.

5 Now Joseph had a dream, and when he told it to his brothers they hated him even more. 6 He said to them, "Hear this dream that I have dreamed: 7 Behold, we were binding sheaves in the field, and behold, my sheaf arose and stood upright. And behold, your sheaves gathered around it and bowed down to my sheaf." 8 His brothers said to him, "Are you indeed to reign over us? Or are you indeed to rule over us?" So they hated him even more for his dreams and for his words.

9 Then he dreamed another dream and told it to his brothers and said, "Behold, I have dreamed another dream. Behold, the sun, the moon, and eleven stars were bowing down to me." 10 But when he told it to his father and to his brothers, his father rebuked him and said to him, "What is this dream that you have dreamed? Shall I and your mother and your brothers indeed come to bow ourselves to the ground before you?" 11 And his

> *brothers were jealous of him, but his father kept the saying in mind.*

Our story began with Joseph as a tell-tale; the young seventeen year old whom God had great plans for. However, much had yet to take place in his life before he would ascend to the exalted position God had in mind for him. To be ready, and he wasn't at this time, thirteen years would pass, full of situations and circumstances that would test and try him to the limit. Patience, isolation, suffering, trust and the polishing of this rough diamond would all reach a new and purifying level. Joseph would soon enter the school of God which would shape and mould him; step by step and moment by moment, in ways never expected and certainly not desired, he would engage with the reality of a life being prepared by God. His lessons would not be learned in the solitude of some distant monastic or theological institution, but at the coalface of life, where mistrust, lies, deceit, spiritual darkness and heathenistic worship were the norm.

Having noted Joseph's first flaw we now come face to face with his fathers. In verse 3 we read: *Now Israel (Jacob) loved Joseph more than any other of his sons.* At first glance this would seem to be a lovely touch, but not so, it was a weakness in his father's character. Whilst the expression of love is rarely a bad thing, in this case it was quite unhealthy and had disastrous consequences. Because his love was not equal, it created problems within the family that would cause incredible grief that almost brought about Jacob's death (Genesis 37:34-35).There is no doubt that Jacob loved all his family, but especially Joseph and Benjamin who were born to Rachel (his first love) in his old age, but it would seem that Jacob recognised something different or special about Joseph that caused him to be unwise by making him a favourite. Joseph must have displayed some quite distinctive attributes (at least potentially) in contrast to his brothers for Jacob to single him out.

Jacob's favouritism is further endorsed by making Joseph a richly ornamented robe (verse 3). He did what he thought was a good thing, but it did Joseph no favours at all. Jacob was old and should have had wisdom in accordance with his years; he had many year's experience as a father, yet this act demonstrates how blind his love for Joseph was. Surely he should have recognised the danger in doing such a thing. His problem was not that he loved – but that his love was not equal. There is a lesson in this; maturity in years does not necessarily guarantee wisdom. We never stop learning. This coat did four things. 1) It revealed Jacob's weakness. 2) It encouraged Joseph's pride. 3) It attracted hatred from his brothers. 4) It meant that the brother's relationship with their father would probably be damaged.

It was one thing for Jacob to give Joseph this spectacular coat, but quite another for him to wear it. Perhaps Joseph should have said, 'no father, I can't possibly wear that coat, what will the others think? I appreciate it but please don't make me wear it'. However, Joseph was quite happy to wear this coat. He had been a spoiled child, which often leads to arrogance. He was insensitive to his brothers` feelings. It seems that he was pleased to swank about flaunting his new acquisition. How did this affect his brothers? *But when his brothers saw that their father loved him more than all his brothers, they hated him and could not speak peacefully to him* (verse 4). Is it any wonder? The coat made a statement to them and incurred the expected response - hatred! The coat told them everything, probably what they already expected but now it was clear for all to see - Jacob loved Joseph more than any of them. It is no surprise, then, that it drove them to silence; they couldn't even muster up a kind word between them. Just to look at Joseph pained them.

Jacob and Joseph were making their mistakes - yet God was in it all! Both men would learn from the error of their ways and eventually benefit from them. In this, we are reminded that our God is a God of grace and mercy and doesn't write us off because of our sins and weaknesses. God was with Joseph and there was no impediment, indiscretion or difficulty that he could not deal with which would bring a halt to his great purpose. The presence of God was the key to Joseph's life. With all that he was and was not, Joseph clearly loved and worshipped God. With the passing of the years it would become evident from Joseph's life that he was pliable to the Spirit of God and submitted to change. His life is a picture of transformation.

Although Joseph got off to a seemingly bad start, we must note that hardly has the narrative started than we are introduced to the fact that he had a gift. He had a God-given gift of receiving and interpreting dreams. These dreams were from God. Although he was young and immature he was still the recipient of divine communication; God was most certainly with him. In the years to come these gifts would be the means of saving his life and also that of his family. Indeed, they would also be instrumental in the formation of a nation. At this point in the story there is a lesson for all Christians. God gives his children gifts, they might not be the ones we want, or would choose, but it is our responsibility to discover them, develop them and use them for his glory and purpose; not for self exaltation.

The dreamer is not yet ready. Joseph had a coat, now he has dreams! Everyone saw the coat; now in his immaturity he tells his brothers that he has had a dream. He just couldn't wait to tell them! Can you imagine this? His brothers already held him in contempt and couldn't speak to him, what are they going to think about his new boast? Verses 5 and 8 tell us that *they hated him even more.* Surprise, surprise! Whether Joseph was arrogant and proud or simply insensitive and immature we cannot tell. One thing is certain - although it may have seemed premature to speak of his dream, the fact remains that it was in keeping with God's purpose and an integral part in this great drama.

Joseph was exalting himself, not just because of the content of the dream but by the very fact that he has received a dream; and obviously from God. In verse 6 he says *Hear this dream that I have dreamed.* Yes, Joseph had a gift but he was not yet ready. In verse 7 the intention is surely to exalt himself above his brothers: *my sheaf rose and stood upright. And behold, your sheaves gathered around it and bowed down to my sheaf.* You and I can understand the accuracy and significance of this dream, but at that time it simply fuelled further hatred with his brothers who had no idea of the future fulfilment of Joseph's dreams. The brothers, however, immediately latched on to the meaning of his dream: *Are you indeed to reign over us? Or are you indeed to rule over us?*

Joseph's gift was there but he wasn't ready to use it for God's glory. Many of God's children may think that because they have a gift they must get on with things and use it - but like Joseph they may not be ready. God often has a lot of polishing and rough edges to knock off before we are ready. This is a sanctifying process that can often take a long time. In Joseph's case it took thirteen years. This illustration is helpful: 'A sculptor was going to make a horse out of a big block of marble and somebody came along to him and said, 'How are you going to do that? He replied, 'It's simple, I just start chipping away and I chip away anything that doesn't look like a horse'. This is how God often deals with us, so long as we place ourselves in his hands.

In verses 9-11 we discover that Joseph has another dream. You would think that he would have learned from his first experience not to fuel the already existing fire – but not so! He now has a second dream and can't wait to tell them, only this time he goes a bit further. He dreamt that *the sun, the moon, and eleven stars were bowing down* to him. They got the message, only this time it included his father and mother bowing down to him. Joseph not only told his brothers but also his father; a step too far. In response his father rebuked him (verse 10).

Although Jacob rebuked Joseph he must surely have recognised that there was something special about this son. It was obvious, even at that time that God was with him. The recipient of a gift will always be responsible as to how they use it. This was a lesson Joseph would learn through the difficult years to come. Perhaps even during times when he might even question the presence or purpose of God. Fine tuning was necessary. As expected, his brothers continued in hatred and were jealous of him (verse 11). Amidst this scene we read: *but his father kept the saying in mind.* He couldn't understand it all but sensed that something special was taking place; and so rather than dismiss the event he kept these things in his heart. This was also true of our Lord's earthly mother, Mary, who did not fully understand what her young son was saying at that time. We read: *And his mother treasured up all these things in her heart* (Luke 2:50-51).

To be fair to Joseph, he was only seventeen at this time, yet so far, it would seem that he had made three mistakes. Firstly, he was a tell-tale. Secondly, he exalted himself with the coat and gifts. Thirdly, he abused his God-given gift. That Joseph still needed much refining in God's sanctifying wheel is clear from the fact that he made the same mistake twice, but don't we all!

But there is a question that must be asked: why did God continue to give Joseph these dreams when he knew it would cause trouble in the family? Humanly speaking Joseph was out of order and unwise, yet in a way that is difficult to understand - God was at work! This is the great anomaly. God is so wonderfully gracious and understanding. In Psalm

103:14 we read: *For he knows our frame, he remembers that we are dust.* We don't have to be perfect to be used by God. From the moment of our spiritual birth and entrance into the Kingdom of God, as his children, even in our spiritual infancy, we are useable in God's hands. This story helps us to see how much God understands us, even with all our weaknesses and mistakes and still wants to use us.

Whilst it is God's purpose that we continue to grow up into spiritual maturity, he doesn't have to wait for that time to come before he uses our gifts and talents. Throughout the varying stages in Joseph's journey, God was with him. It is not so much our ability or inability that God is interested in - but our availability! Joseph was available. He had a heart for God that kept him trusting even in the darkest times. Dr R T Kendall writes: 'Joseph was God's diamond in the rough. He needed a lot of polishing before his time would come. But that is the way God sees each of us - diamonds that no one around us would recognize. It's what God sees that matters.'

CHAPTER 3

The experience of the pit

Genesis 37:12-26

12 Now his brothers went to pasture their father's flock near Shechem. 13 And Israel said to Joseph, "Are not your brothers pasturing the flock at Shechem? Come, I will send you to them." And he said to him, "Here I am." 14 So he said to him, "Go now, see if it is well with your brothers and with the flock, and bring me word." So he sent him from the Valley of Hebron, and he came to Shechem. 15 And a man found him wandering in the fields. And the man asked him, "What are you seeking?" 16 "I am seeking my brothers," he said. "Tell me, please, where they are pasturing the flock." 17 And the man said, "They have gone away, for I heard them say, 'Let us go to Dothan.' " So Joseph went after his brothers and found them at Dothan.
18 They saw him from afar, and before he came near to them they conspired against him to kill him. 19 They said to one another, "Here comes this dreamer. 20 Come now, let us kill him and throw him into one of the pits. Then we will say that a fierce animal has devoured him, and we will see what will become of his dreams." 21 But when Reuben heard it, he rescued him out of their hands, saying, "Let us not take his life." 22 And Reuben said to them, "Shed no blood; cast him into this pit here in the wilderness, but do not lay a hand on

him"— that he might rescue him out of their hand to restore him to his father. 23 So when Joseph came to his brothers, they stripped him of his robe, the robe of many colours that he wore. 24 And they took him and cast him into a pit. The pit was empty; there was no water in it.

25 Then they sat down to eat. And looking up they saw a caravan of Ishmaelites coming from Gilead, with their camels bearing gum, balm, and myrrh, on their way to carry it down to Egypt. 26 Then Judah said to his brothers, "What profit is it if we kill our brother and conceal his blood?

We have already looked at Joseph's early life; noting his faults, gifts, immaturity and his self righteousness. Jacob, his father, also demonstrated favouritism and the danger of an unequal love. This created terrible tension and rivalry within the family; for we are told that the brothers *hated him and could not speak peacefully to him* (verse 4). They were driven to silence. In spite of this, however, God's sovereign purpose was never absent.

Having a gift does not necessarily mean that it's ready for immediate use. God's gifts to his children will invariably go through stages of development and maturing. As already pointed out, thirteen years of fine tuning, suffering and testing lay ahead before the true value of God's gift to Joseph would be seen. We may recall that God allowed this with Moses - only it took forty years before the man in Egypt, brimming with confidence and passion, would be ready. Yes! It took forty years of solitude, shepherding and reflection before Moses, in all humility and stripped of his self-confidence could say, *'who am I?* (Exodus 3:11). Having experienced the waywardness and unpredictability of sheep, he was about to discover similar characteristics as he led the children of Israel out of slavery and into the promised land. Moses was now ready (but not perfect). In his weakness he would discover God's power.

From verses 12-13 we note that Jacob did what might be considered to be a very unwise thing. He decided to send Joseph to his brothers to check that all was well and bring a report back to him. Knowing that Joseph's relationship with his brothers was at breaking point; for they hated him and couldn't even speak to him - why did Jacob decide to send Joseph to them? Was this not asking for trouble? It is also remarkable that Joseph was willing to do what his father had requested: in spite of what may have awaited him, he acted in obedience to his father. This was commendable. At a human level, it may be that Jacob thought the brothers would cool off and that Joseph would be a little more cautious with his tongue. We can't be certain. The only thing we can be sure about is that it was all part of God's sovereign purpose; a glorious theme woven throughout this wonderful piece of history.

When Jacob sent Joseph off he had no idea just how long it would be before he would see his face again. Ahead lay years of mourning and sadness, times of sleepless nights and unanswered questions. Yet he must also have clung on to God's great purpose in spite of all the uncertainties. The Christian life can be like this; in times of difficulty and trial, when questions are many and answers few - we must remain resolute and faithful, believing that our God has the measure of all things in his hands. Arranging the circumstances and events of his people are part of God's wonderful plan - although we don't always see it like that (Romans 8:28). Perhaps it's just as well that we don't know what lies ahead; it makes sense to live just one day at a time.

Having travelled to Shechem and not finding his brothers there, he enquired of a stranger (arranged by God) about their whereabouts and was told that they had moved on to Dothan. Joseph now drew near to Dothan where his brothers were to be found. It has to be said that by travelling to such remote and dangerous parts, especially on his own, Joseph put himself at great risk.

In verse 18 we read: *They saw him from afar, and before he came near to them they conspired against him to kill him.* Their hatred was still there; perhaps worse than ever, they hadn't cooled off. What did they see as they caught sight of Joseph? That coat! It may be that Joseph was swaggering along flaunting this coat of contention. After what had happened, you would have thought the coat would have been cast aside - but not so. Before Joseph reached them, in almost an instant, and referring to him as 'that dreamer', they decided to kill him and throw him into a pit. As though murdering your own brother wasn't enough, they also worked out their alibi. Perhaps even more so than the coat, it was Joseph's dreams that really stuck in their throat, because they said: *and we will see what becomes of his dreams* (verse 20). The thought of them one day bowing down before Joseph was more than they could bear.

One of the brothers, Reuben, who was the eldest, heard what the others had in mind and obviously did not want to be part of it, so he made another suggestion. He didn't want them to kill Joseph but to leave him in the pit, so that some time later he could rescue him and take him back to his father. Later in the story we find that Reuben is horrified to discover that in his absence the other brothers had sold Joseph as a slave. We are told that *he tore his clothes* (verse 29), a sign of his grief. It may be that as the eldest brother Reuben should have used his authority and resisted the evil plot – but, for whatever reason, it seems that he couldn't bring himself to do that.

Not surprisingly, the first thing the brothers did when Joseph arrived was to rip that coat from his back - they just couldn't wait! Then they dumped him into the pit. What we discover next is quite unthinkable. We are informed in verse 25 that they sat down to eat. How could they? They are so callous and hard hearted, totally insensitive to the situation. They were prepared to leave Joseph to die, probably of thirst within a few days since there was no water in the pit, whilst they relaxed and sat down to a meal. Sinfulness and a hard heart can allow people to do such things. According to 42: 21 Joseph begged for mercy.

During his time in the pit, I wonder what Joseph was thinking about! Imagine him in that dried out water well. Was he questioning his dreams? Did he even doubt God's revelation to him? Where were his dreams now? Were they in tatters, had God abandoned him? How he was feeling we just don't know; but one thing's for sure, when you are in a pit there is only one way you can look - and that's up! Perhaps Joseph looked up and cried unto God. This was Job's experience. Read Job 23:8-10.

When God puts his hand upon us – it will change us! It will not always be the way we want: but it will be personal and unique. What God was about to do for Joseph had never been done before and Joseph could not look back at some other situation for encouragement, guidance or hope, he had just to keep on trusting. God was chastening Joseph – not to get even with him but to prepare him for the future.

At times we may wonder what's going on in our lives, we might question God and say, what's going on Lord? Why is this happening to me? Like Joseph, if we truly want God's hand to continue upon us we must keep trusting: I am of the opinion that Joseph was still trusting in his God. In Joseph's life we read on several occasions that the Lord was with him (Chapter 39:2, 21, 23). Why does God allow us to be in the pit at times? So that we might be able to see what God can do for us when there's no way out. We must come to the end of ourselves before there's room for God to work. Listen to

Joseph's words as he stands before Pharaoh: *It is not in me ... God will give* (Chapter 41:16).

At this point it's worth highlighting a few of the many similarities (which must not be stretched too far) between Jesus and Joseph.

- Jesus came with good news as the Saviour. Men could not understand and cried, crucify him. Joseph came to his family with the news that one day he would be their saviour from famine and starvation. The brothers said kill him.
- Jesus said I am your King, your Sovereign but the people said we will not have this man to rule over us. Joseph said through his dreams that one day he would be their sovereign, ruling over them and that they would bow down before him.
- Jesus was put on the cross at the hands of men, they thought they were in charge – but God was in it. Joseph's brothers thought they were in control - but it was God.
- Jesus was nailed to the cross and died - but God raised him. Joseph was put into the pit, but God planned for the Ishmaelites to pass that way, and Joseph was raised again.
- Jesus betrayed for cash - Joseph sold for cash.

How wonderful God's sovereign purpose is. Earlier, Joseph was met by a stranger who redirected him to where the brothers had gone; now the Ishmaelites arrive just at the right time. Luck, chance, coincidence; certainly not! God was at work. Judah, one of the brothers, now has second thoughts and suggests that they don't leave Joseph to die, but should sell him to the Ishmaelites. Remembering that Joseph is his brother, his own flesh and blood, Judah softens a little. And so this new suggestion met with the approval of the others and Joseph is sold to them for twenty shekels of silver. They set out for Egypt where he would be sold as a slave.

During this time, Reuben had been attending to other duties and was not party to the selling of Joseph to the Ishmaelites; he expected to come back and remove Joseph from the pit with a mind to have him returned to his father. He is devastated to discover Joseph's absence and what had happened. In response he went back to his brothers and tore his clothes as an expression of grief, saying: *The boy is gone, and I, where shall I go?* (verse 29).

What followed defies even common cruelty. They slaughtered a goat and dipped Joseph's robe into it, no doubt also tearing it apart as part of their deception. How could they possibly take this to their father knowing that the shock of Joseph's (supposed) savage death could kill him? Imagine them laying this bloodstained coat before their father and inviting him to examine it! How cruel is this, allowing Jacob to think that Joseph had been torn apart by some wild animal?

One sin leads to another, and in this case, gross insensitivity is the result. We cannot begin to understand how Jacob felt. Like Reuben earlier, he too, tore his clothes and entered into mourning. During this time he may even have questioned his own judgement. Should he have sent Joseph on such a perilous journey? Was Jacob guilt ridden? The depth of Jacob's grief is seen by declaring that his mourning would never leave him until his own death. Jacob's sons and daughters gathered around to comfort him - including those responsible for this deception - what a sight? But Jacob refused to be comforted.

So far, there would seem to be nothing promising about this story. Other than Joseph's gifts, albeit in his immaturity, we see favouritism, jealousy, attempted murder, deceit and hatred. Yet, in ways we cannot understand, God was working out his sovereign purpose on a scale beyond measure. Goodness and glory, deliverance for famine stricken nations and the emergence of a new nation, Israel, would come into being. For all this to take place, Joseph had to be removed from home and taken to Egypt. The script could not have been written as to how this would be done. The key player in all of this had much to learn; Joseph had now entered thirteen years of polishing and reshaping. Darkness and despair, as well as promising times lay ahead before he would eventually be ready. How encouraging then, to remember that in all of this, God was at work. Romans 8:28 *And we know that for those who love God all things work together for good, for those who are called according to his purpose.*

CHAPTER 4

A new beginning in Egypt

Genesis 39:1-23

Now Joseph had been brought down to Egypt, and Potiphar, an officer of Pharaoh, the captain of the guard, an Egyptian, had bought him from the Ishmaelites who had brought him down there. 2 The Lord was with Joseph, and he became a successful man, and he was in the house of his Egyptian master. 3 His master saw that the Lord was with him and that the Lord caused all that he did to succeed in his hands. 4 So Joseph found favour in his sight and attended him, and he made him overseer of his house and put him in charge of all that he had. 5 From the time that he made him overseer in his house and over all that he had the Lord blessed the Egyptian's house for Joseph's sake; the blessing of the Lord was on all that he had, in house and field. 6 So he left all that he had in Joseph's charge, and because of him he had no concern about anything but the food he ate.
Now Joseph was handsome in form and appearance. 7 And after a time his master's wife cast her eyes on Joseph and said, "Lie with me." 8 But he refused and said to his master's wife, "Behold, because of me my master has no concern about anything in the house, and he has put everything that he has in my charge. 9 He is not greater in this house than I am, nor has he kept

back anything from me except yourself, because you are his wife. How then can I do this great wickedness and sin against God?" 10 And as she spoke to Joseph day after day, he would not listen to her, to lie beside her or to be with her.

11 But one day, when he went into the house to do his work and none of the men of the house was there in the house, 12 she caught him by his garment, saying, "Lie with me." But he left his garment in her hand and fled and got out of the house. 13 And as soon as she saw that he had left his garment in her hand and had fled out of the house, 14 she called to the men of her household and said to them, "See, he has brought among us a Hebrew to laugh at us. He came in to me to lie with me, and I cried out with a loud voice. 15 And as soon as he heard that I lifted up my voice and cried out, he left his garment beside me and fled and got out of the house." 16 Then she laid up his garment by her until his master came home, 17 and she told him the same story, saying, "The Hebrew servant, whom you have brought among us, came in to me to laugh at me. 18 But as soon as I lifted up my voice and cried, he left his garment beside me and fled out of the house."

19 As soon as his master heard the words that his wife spoke to him, "This is the way your servant treated me," his anger was kindled. 20 And Joseph's master took him and put him into the prison, the place where the king's prisoners were confined, and he was there in prison. 21 But the Lord was with Joseph and showed him steadfast love and gave him favour in the sight of the keeper of the prison. 22 And the keeper of the prison put Joseph in charge of all the prisoners who were in the prison. Whatever was done there, he was the one who did it. 23 The keeper of the prison paid no attention to anything that was in Joseph's charge, because the Lord was with him. And whatever he did, the Lord made it succeed.

We now find Joseph having been taken to Egypt by the Ishmaelites and sold as a slave to Potiphar, who was one of Pharaoh's officials and a captain of his guard. He is now in phase two of his preparation for God's future purpose and moves for the time being from riches to rags. God continues to arrange the circumstances of his life, although Joseph is no doubt unaware of exactly why all this has happened to him. Yet it is clear that amidst this dark and unsettled period, Joseph continued to trust and believe. Not easy to do!

Joseph's circumstances now radically change. From wanting for nothing under the spoiling eye of his father, where he never lacked for anything, he has now been transported in a most degrading and heart-wrenching fashion and sold into servant-hood as a slave. He is now compelled to submit to a lifestyle quite foreign to him. There would be no family worship taking place in his new pagan environment. Physical, spiritual and emotional readjustments would take place as he learned to cope in his new surroundings. We must remember that at this time he was just seventeen. Joseph would never have chosen to leave family and friends and go to another country, yet in the greater purpose of God this had to happen, though it seemed cruel at the time.

Joseph is alone, yet not alone. The best company anyone can have is God - this was certainly true of Joseph. Verse 2 tells us: *The Lord was with Joseph.* Everything else may have been left behind but not the presence of God. But how are we to understand this verse? In what sense was the Lord with Joseph; what did it mean to him? Consider the following.

- In his private devotions he would know God's nearness.
- He would receive strength to maintain his integrity and moral uprightness.
- Amidst an ungodly environment he would receive assurance and a future hope.
- He would be guided daily in all his duties and responsibilities.
- He would receive wisdom from above that would bring great success.

How do we know that the Lord was with Joseph? Because it was visible for all to see! There was something about his appearance, his words and his ways, that stood out from all others. In spite of his young age and immaturity the reality of God's presence penetrated that heathen environment as light in a dark place. Not only was Joseph *successful* (verse 2), but his master saw that he *succeeded* in everything that he did (verse 3). Potiphar noted that Joseph's success stood in contrast to the achievements of those around him; this was God at work! Clearly, then, Joseph was a marked man because the Lord was with him. How wonderful and encouraging it is to see that even in the most adverse circumstances the witness of God's presence can be in evidence. Perhaps God's presence was deeper and more meaningful than before, because while Joseph was back home he had his father and family to lean on – but now there was only God! To know this new experience he had to be away from home; leave his past, and learn to trust God with the future.

What were the results of the Lord being with Joseph? From verses 3-6 we find that Potiphar, his master, was quick to recognise that his success found its source in the Lord: *His master saw that the Lord was with him and that the Lord caused all that he did to succeed in his hands.* Nothing escaped the Lord's blessing; everything Joseph did was blessed with great success. Not only were Joseph's activities blessed, but we are informed in verse 5 that the Lord also *blessed the Egyptian's house for Joseph's sake.* Here we have the righteousness of God spilling over into a dark ungodly world. Jesus taught that believers were to be 'salt and light' in this world: and that's exactly what Joseph was centuries before Jesus uttered those words. As a result of this, Potiphar promoted Joseph and he became his personal attendant, putting him in charge of his entire household. That Joseph greatly impressed Potiphar is seen in that he gave him responsibility over 'everything' except the food he ate.

Joseph was a means of blessing to those around him and successful in all his responsibilities. His light burned brightly as a testimony to the living God. His example provides us with a glowing illustration of just how our faith and faithfulness can impact this godless age in which we live. God looks for men and women today whose walk with him is so intimate that the life of our Saviour becomes visible. In Acts 4:13 when Peter and John were brought before the Jewish hierarchy to be questioned for preaching the gospel; we read: *And they recognized that they had been with Jesus.* Is this not a reminder to all Christians that our mandate is not only to declare the gospel in word but also by our demeanour? *And we all, with unveiled face, beholding the glory of the Lord, are being transformed into the same image from one degree of glory to another. For this comes from the Lord who is the Spirit* (2 Corinthians 3:18). It was St Francis of Assisi (1181-1226 AD) who said, 'Preach the gospel at all times, if necessary - use words.'

Joseph was making much progress; now it was time for him to be tested. The late G B Duncan comments: 'Jesus was tempted, not because he was bad, but because he was important.' Although to a lesser extent, this was true of Joseph. Satan is never idle; he is the antagonist and enemy of God and all who believe. He will do everything and anything to thwart the purpose of God. In the Old Testament book of

Job we discover that Satan's onslaught was not set against someone who was a spiritual failure or had sinned badly. No! His target was that of a righteous man who is described in Job 1:1 in this way: This man was *blameless and upright; one who feared God and turned away from evil.*

And so, Joseph, although still a young man and far from perfect - became a target for Satan. God had much planned for him; more than ever he could have imagined. Even though his earlier dreams with their interpretations had pointed to his exalted future status; at that time he could not have understood their full significance. One day he would govern Egypt with only Pharaoh above him. Satan now seeks to bring Joseph down, and with him, disrupt the future purpose of God.

Verse 6 tells us that Joseph was *handsome in form and appearance.* Satan is not blind! His good looks and physique were to be the target for Satan's scheming. Joseph hadn't gone unnoticed to Potiphar's wife. Perhaps Joseph was vulnerable, being away from home without family and friends and no reputation to defend. Satan was about to use the oldest trick in the book in his endeavours to make shipwreck of Joseph's life. This would tell us what was really in Joseph's heart. Would he resist temptation? Would he have the strength to flee from it? Would this young man be able to stand against the subtlety and scheming of the evil one? Would he submit to the pressure of the occasion? This was a tough one for Joseph! Had he failed, God's purpose could have been in tatters and his life ruined.

Joseph passed the test with flying colours - he triumphed over sexual temptation. He won the battle because God mattered more to him than anything else, including sexual gratification. How did he respond? Joseph made a point blank refusal to the invitation of Potiphar's wife. He did not flirt in his mind or play with the idea because he knew that there was no future in travelling down that road. This was wrong and harmful and only disaster awaited him should he have yielded. Notice please; this was no fleeting temptation. We read in verse 10: *And as she spoke to Joseph day after day, he would not listen to her, to lie beside her or to be with her.* She persisted and pestered him, yet his resolve was equal to the occasion. Such was the pressure set against him that after having determined in his mind what was right to do, he *fled and got out of the house* (verse 12). He fled from her continual badgering and got as much distance between the two of them as possible. Richard De Haan once wrote: 'If you want to avoid eating the forbidden fruit then stay away from the devil's orchard'.

We are now to discover the secret of Joseph's strength. It was his sensitivity and submission to a holy and righteous God. In verse 9 Joseph says: *How then can I do this great wickedness and sin against God?* This is surely the level of devotion that God requires for all who would follow him. Should Joseph have failed the test and sinned, this would have been a sin against Potiphar's wife, Potiphar and himself, yet it would have been far more serious than this, and Joseph knew it.

It would have been first and foremost a sin against God. Following King David's adultery with Bathsheba, in his prayer of repentance in Psalm 51:4 he says: *Against you, you only have I sinned and done what is evil in your sight.* The same was true of the prodigal son; when he decided to return home to his father, we read in Luke 15:18 what he planned to say: *Father, I have sinned against heaven and before you.* Once again, just like Joseph and David, he realised that sin would always be firstly an offence against God. Joseph faced a real test in this temptation. God had plans for him and the development of those plans called for Joseph to face tests. Joseph proved by his response that God was not only with him, but was also the source of his power and his reason for not sinning. Throughout the Joseph story we find that he faced many tests. These were all part of the making of the man, these helped him to know himself and prove that the purpose of God was more important to him than anything else. God's sanctifying process with all its testings and trials would continue, until the time came, when Joseph was truly ready.

Faithfulness to God, however, does not necessarily guarantee an easy or pleasant path through life, as Joseph was about to discover. Potiphar's wife did not run into a corner and lick her wounds; far from it! Instead, she is determined to bring Joseph down and holds on to Joseph's cloak as he fled the scene. Earlier in Joseph's story his coat was taken from him by his brothers, now it is his cloak. The first was used as evidence of his supposed death, the second to falsely accuse him of rape.

This woman went from one sin to another in order to justify her failed attempt at seduction. But Satan doesn't give up without a fight! She became a liar and a deceiver in her endeavours to convince her servants and her husband that Joseph had tried to have an affair with her (verses 14-18). Sin has no lower limits and Satan will do anything and use anybody to discredit and bring the purpose of God to a halt. He will wreck lives and disrupt congregations, anything to further his cause. In the book of Job 1:7 we read: *The Lord said to Satan, 'Where have you come from?' Satan answered the Lord and said, 'From going to and fro on the earth and from walking up and down on it.* Another way of expressing this would be, 'I've been everywhere and anywhere'. Satan is always looking for evil opportunities.

Potiphar had little option but to act on the basis of his wife's lies, even though he may have had his own doubts – we'll never know! Joseph's response is one of silence; Scripture says nothing of Joseph making any attempt to justify or vindicate himself. To do so may only have made matters worse. God knew the truth, and Joseph settled for that. He cast himself into the hands of God. Just like our Saviour in Matthew 27:14 Joseph made no reply, not even to a single charge. Joseph in this respect was like Christ. The apostle Peter expresses it this way in 1 Peter 2:19 (NIV): *For it is commendable if a man bears up under pain of unjust suffering because he is conscious of God.* In a sense Joseph passed an important test, part of his continual preparation before being used by God. It was this: although being punished for doing well, he was able to keep quiet about it. In due course and with the passing of time God would bring about his vindication.

In verse 20 we read: *Joseph's master took him and put him into the prison, the place where the King's prisoners were confined.* It wasn't just any old cell, but an inner dungeon - a high security cell. What a journey life was bringing up for Joseph! From a favourite son to a slave; from a slave to a servant; and now from being the head of a household - to a prisoner. How difficult it must have been for Joseph to be patient, especially since he was entirely innocent. God's great purpose must have seemed very cruel at this stage - yet God was using every circumstance and event for his greater glory and the future exaltation and blessing of Joseph; though at this time Joseph was oblivious to all this. Joseph was being pruned and shaped; his character moulded step by step until the time of his restoration.

It is not surprising that three times in this chapter we read that *The Lord was with Joseph* (Verses 2, 21, 23). These words are a fitting title for the whole of Joseph's life. The sovereign purpose of God is woven through the entire narrative as we witness God at work in this young man's life. There never was a time when Joseph was alone; his Lord was constantly with him. This was King David's experience also, for we read in Psalm 139:7-10: *Where shall I go from your Spirit? Or where shall I flee from your presence? If I ascend to heaven, you are there. If I make my bed in Sheol, you are there! If I take the wings of the morning and dwell in the uttermost parts of the sea, even there your hand shall lead me, and your right hand shall hold me.* How encouraging to remember that we have a God who has promised never to leave us or forsake us. Through sunshine and sorrow he will be with us, even our darkest moments will not be in isolation, for just as the *Lord was with Joseph* so he will be with those who love him and seek out his purpose.

This chapter concludes with evidence that the Lord was with Joseph, for very soon after entering prison he caught the attention of the prison warder. This is not surprising, it was the story of Joseph's life - the presence of the Lord caused him to be a marked man in the most positive way. The result being that Joseph was promoted to a position of responsibility. Why was Joseph promoted? Why was he successful? Verse 23 provides the answer: *because the Lord was with him. And whatever he did, the Lord made it succeed.* In this heathen environment Joseph must have stood head and shoulders above his fellow prisoners - a bright light in a dark place. Such is the challenge for all believers. Jesus not only said that he was the Light of the world, but also said to his followers: *You are the light of the world* (Matthew 5:14).

CHAPTER 5

God moves in mysterious ways

Genesis 40:1-23

Some time after this, the cupbearer of the king of Egypt and his baker committed an offence against their lord the king of Egypt. 2 And Pharaoh was angry with his two officers, the chief cupbearer and the chief baker, 3 and he put them in custody in the house of the captain of the guard, in the prison where Joseph was confined. 4 The captain of the guard appointed Joseph to be with them, and he attended them. They continued for some time in custody.

5 And one night they both dreamed—the cupbearer and the baker of the king of Egypt, who were confined in the prison–each his own dream, and each dream with its own interpretation. 6 When Joseph came to them in the morning, he saw that they were troubled. 7 So he asked Pharaoh's officers who were with him in custody in his master's house, "Why are your faces downcast today?" 8 They said to him, "We have had dreams, and there is no one to interpret them." And Joseph said to them, "Do not interpretations belong to God? Please tell them to me." 9 So the chief cupbearer told his dream to Joseph and said to him, "In my dream there was a vine before me, 10 and on the vine there were three branches. As soon as it budded, its blossoms shot forth, and the clusters ripened into grapes. 11 Pharaoh's cup was in my hand, and I took the grapes and pressed them into Pharaoh's cup and placed the cup in Pharaoh's hand." 12 Then Joseph said to him, "This is its interpretation: the three branches are three days. 13 In three days Pharaoh will lift up your head and restore you to your office, and you shall place Pharaoh's cup in his hand as formerly, when you were his cupbearer. 14 Only remember me, when it is well with you, and please do me the kindness to mention me to Pharaoh, and so get me out of this house. 15 For I was indeed stolen out of the land of the Hebrews, and here also I have done nothing that they should put me into the pit."

16 When the chief baker saw that the interpretation was favourable, he said to Joseph, "I also had a dream: there were three cake baskets on my head, 17 and in the uppermost basket there were all sorts of baked food for Pharaoh, but the birds were eating it out of the basket on my head." 18 And Joseph answered and said, "This is its interpretation: the three baskets are three days. 19 In three days Pharaoh will lift up your head—from you!—and hang you on a tree. And the birds will eat the flesh from you."

20 On the third day, which was Pharaoh's birthday, he made a feast for all his servants and lifted up the head of the chief cupbearer and the head of the chief baker among his servants. 21 He restored the chief cupbearer to his position, and he placed the cup in Pharaoh's hand. 22 But he hanged the chief baker, as Joseph had interpreted to them. 23 Yet the chief cupbearer did not remember Joseph, but forgot him.

For the time being, it may seem that Joseph's world has once again collapsed. In spite of his innocence and even though he has been promoted - he is still a prisoner and not at liberty to live as he would have chosen. As we shall see later, being in prison was God-ordained, because if Potiphar had really believed Joseph to be guilty, surely he would have been executed; thereby bringing a premature end to this most glorious story and God's wonderful plan regarding the creation of Israel as a nation.

We see, however, a principle at work in Joseph's life which equally applies to all true believers who want nothing but God's purpose for their lives. What is this principle? That God often uses various types of trials, tests, adverse situations and circumstances which we would never have chosen - yet God uses them, not as a punishment for sins or disobedience, or to get even with us (he doesn't do that), but for our sanctification and preparation for his future purpose. This process does two things: it makes us more holy and more useable in God's service. During this period in Joseph's life we'll never know how many times he questioned God or made it clear that he felt as though he had had enough. Perhaps there were times when he uttered words similar to that of our Lord: *My God, my God why have you forsaken me?* (Matthew 27:46). Like God's servant Job, he had no idea the reason or the purpose in it all.

In chapter 39 we left Joseph gaining success in his new responsibilities in prison. Now in the opening verse of chapter 40 we find four words of great significance: *Some time after this.* One of the most difficult things to do in life is to have patience; to wait. The temptation is often to take the initiative or instigate action because we just want to get things done, thereby removing uncertainty from situations.

Maturity is always a process. It is not possible for apples to grow overnight or flowers to spring into glorious bloom a few hours after the seed is sown. Nor is it possible in education for the pupil to be catapulted into a teaching position before they have patiently and diligently grown in knowledge and experience (even although the potential is there). In this we have a parallel within Christian experience. Spiritual growth takes time and calls for commitment, devotion and patience. It also calls for our trust in the purpose of God, for it is not uncommon for Christians to think that their gift is not being used and that opportunity to use their gift is passing them by. Too often we are 'not' as ready as we think!

In Joseph's case, *some time after this* probably meant about one year later. Another year of preparation and pruning! Preparation is not so painful if you know the reason for it or have planned it, but not knowing is often what makes it hard. The great consolation in all this (although we don't see it at the time) is that God deals with all his children so personally and individually. He is the master planner who sets in motion the shaping of our lives, just one step at a time. Each step may involve some trial or chastening before we can move on. God knows what we can stand; he knows what we can and can't bear and never takes us beyond what we're able to endure. 1 Corinthians 10:13b ... *And all you need to remember is that God will never let you down; he'll never let you be pushed past your limit; he'll always be there to help you come through it* (The Message – Eugene H Peterson).

This whole and lengthy process involved Joseph changing. Two gems are emerging in his life; humility and servanthood. Both these qualities are found in the Lord Jesus Christ in the fullest and deepest measure (see John chapter 13 and Philippians 2:1-11). Back in Canaan these qualities were absent in Joseph's life. However, the time is now right for Joseph's gifts to emerge and play a vital role in the shaping of his future and the unfolding of God's greater purpose.

It begins with Pharaoh's chief cupbearer and chief baker offending their King and being thrown into prison. Pharaoh was very angry with these men who had held very important positions before being banished to the same prison as Joseph. Coincidence: never! God was at work. How remarkable that these men are put under Joseph's charge. You couldn't write the script. Just at that precise moment in history God brought them together, not too soon and not too late.

Back in the jail and after they had been in custody for some time, we learn that the cupbearer and the baker both had dreams on the same night. When Joseph, who had responsibility for them, came in the next morning he found them rather downcast and dejected. Joseph could easily have ignored them but expressed his concern and compassion regarding their troubled spirits. It is lovely to see his genuine interest in others. He said: *Why are your faces downcast today?* (verse 7). They told him that they both had dreams but there was no-one to interpret them. On the other side of the prison door, in their previous situations, they would have called for astrologers to interpret their dreams; this was common and big business. But who could help them in prison?

What a wonderful situation is before Joseph – they had no idea about Joseph's past in relation to his dreams and their interpretation. Can you imagine what was going on inside Joseph? Perhaps he was tempted to say something like; well, I'm your man! I can interpret dreams. But that's not what he said; Joseph was changing and rather than point towards himself he pointed towards God. The opportunity was there for self exaltation, but Joseph said: *Do not interpretations belong to God? Please tell them to me* (verse 8). Years before the young impetuous Joseph may well have sought prominence in such a situation, but not now - he is maturing.

In the midst of this heathen environment he exalts the living God - surely this is evidence that even in such a place as this he was keeping fellowship with God. The Lord was with

Joseph. God gives a great diversity of gifts to his children, yet these gifts will only reach their fullest potential when used to glorify and exalt God (see 1 Peter 4:10-11). In the Westminster Shorter Catechism the first question asked is; 'What is man's chief end? Answer, 'To glorify God and enjoy him forever.' Here is a lesson for all who seek to serve God. On one occasion Dr Martyn Lloyd-Jones attended a conference where two well known speakers each ministered from God's Word. Afterwards, he was asked what he thought of the ministry. He said; 'Both men spoke extremely well, the first left me thinking about how great he was; the other left me thinking of how great Christ was.'

Joseph is now ready to use his gift and so he invites the cupbearer and the baker to tell him their dreams. In verses 9-11 we have details of the cupbearer's dream which is self-explanatory. Joseph's interpretation was great news for the cupbearer; for in three days Joseph said he would be restored to his original position as cupbearer to Pharaoh. The time had arrived for Joseph's gift to be tested. Joseph had committed himself to a certain course of action in a definite period of time. Would it happen? Would Joseph be proved right? He would either show great confidence in God, or look a fool. He now puts his neck on the line for God. He offered nothing other than plan A, no alternatives or other options. Also notice the timescale – three days. Not months or years!

Not only was Joseph's gift put to the test, but his character also comes under scrutiny. For a period of thirteen years Joseph was placed under the watchful eye of God. *And no creature is hidden from his sight, but all are naked and exposed to the eyes of him to whom we must give account.* (Hebrews 4:13) *I am he who searches mind and heart ...* (Revelation 2:23). Trials and tests in Christian experience, though never sought, undoubtedly have their value. Among the many and varied reasons for them, they are often designed to show us something about ourselves that we didn't know, and maybe didn't want to know! Too often, perhaps, we think of ourselves more highly than we ought and don't really see ourselves as we truly are. In John 16:13 we read regarding the work of the Holy Spirit: *When the Spirit of truth comes, he will guide you into all truth* ... Part of this work of the Spirit is to help us see ourselves, to engage in self-examination and respond to what the Spirit has revealed.

Although Joseph was maturing – we now discover a flaw in his character. His success with the interpretation of the cupbearer's dream introduced a moment of weakness. God saw something deep rooted that needed to be dealt with in Joseph's heart. There was still a bit in Joseph that wanted to manipulate his future. In an unguarded moment Joseph said to the cupbearer in verse 14, *Only remember me, when it is well with you, and please do me the kindness to mention me to Pharaoh, and so get me out of this house.* That little word me! In this single verse he used it four times. Joseph saw an opportunity to change his circumstances and perhaps said no more than you or I would have done given a similar situation. Notice also in verse 15 that he tells the cupbearer about his past injustice and ill-treatment. He engages in this form of self-pity hoping that it would enhance his situation. However, God had great plans for Joseph and this form of self-exaltation was not healthy.

Much would be expected of Joseph in the years ahead and it was important that God's refining process continued. Following the restoration of the cupbearer to his former position, it is unfortunate, yet part of God's plan, that according to verse 23 we read: *Yet the chief cupbearer did not remember Joseph, but forgot him.* According to chapter 44:1 it would seem that Joseph's failed attempt cost him two more years in prison – he was not yet ready! Lessons abound in Joseph's story, in particular, to be sensitive to the Holy Spirit as he reveals to us those areas in our lives and unholy deficiencies that call for our attention, so that our spiritual growth and usefulness to God may not be hindered. The work of sanctification is ever progressive and it can often be the seemingly small things (in our eyes) that keep us back. Hebrews 12:1 ... *let us also lay aside every weight, and sin which clings so closely* ... 2 Corinthians 7:1 ... *let us cleanse ourselves from every defilement of body and spirit, bringing holiness to completion in the fear of God.*

As this chapter comes to a conclusion we discover the sad fate of the chief baker. We read in verse 23, *But he hanged the chief baker, as Joseph had interpreted to them.* Following the favourable interpretation given to the cupbearer, the baker probably expected a good result also. The outcome, however, was devastatingly different. He was to be hanged in three days. We can't begin to understand how difficult it must have been for Joseph to be the bearer of such an interpretation. This was surely a great test of Joseph's faithfulness to God's revelation. God's tests are always for a sanctifying purpose: *The Lord tests the righteous* ... (Psalm 11:5). Joseph's future responsibilities in Egypt would call for one who had been well tried and tested. 1 Corinthians 4:2 *Now it is required of those who have been given a trust must prove faithful* (New International Version). Theodore Epp comments, 'Daily faithfulness in ordinary duties is the best preparation for future service.'

Joseph's word to the cupbearer and baker were not, of course, the result of one being restored and the other hanged, he was only the messenger bringing God's word. The outcome was not his responsibility but remained in the purpose of God. Though it might be mere speculation, it would not be surprising if during those three dark days (yet days of grace) before the baker's hanging, that Joseph revealed to him something of the greatness of his God. Furthermore, it is more than likely that Joseph shared the sad news with compassion and love. Only heaven can bear witness to the full influence Joseph may have had with the baker.

Care must be taken not to stretch the point too far, but we see in this situation Joseph as a type of Christ, in particular, as our Lord hung upon the cross with two criminals, one on either side of him. The destination of these men was quite different, one restored into fellowship with God through faith in Christ - the other remained in unbelief and therefore eternally condemned. Joseph was in prison at the hands of men, undeserving to be there and entirely innocent of the charges against him. He finds himself as God's man, being used to communicate the will of God to the cupbearer and the baker interpretations of dreams that would lead one to restoration and the other to death.

For the time being Joseph was the forgotten man by man - but not by God! God was still at work in his life; Joseph was where God wanted him to be for the working out of his greater purpose. Joseph had to learn not to put his trust in man - but in God. *It is better to take refuge in the Lord than to trust in man* (Psalm 118:8). What wonderful advice we find as a rule for life in Proverbs 3:5-6, *Trust in the Lord with all your heart, and do not lean on your own understanding. In all your ways acknowledge him, and he will make straight your paths.*

CHAPTER 6

God's timing is perfect

Genesis 41:1

After two whole years ...

Having suffered the disappointment of being forgotten by
the chief cupbearer (but not by God), Joseph then spent
another two years in prison. He was now paying the price for
his impatience. What Joseph said to the cupbearer about
his past ill-treatment and innocence was all true (Genesis
40:14-15), but it was just not the right time to say it. There is
a lesson to be learned from Joseph's understandable attempt
at securing his own release. It is not always a question of
what or what not to say in any given situation; there are
times when the best course of action is to say nothing. It is
interesting to note, and to his credit, that we have no record
of Joseph defending himself when he stood falsely accused
before Potiphar. The example of the Lord Jesus is pre-eminent
in this respect. *He was oppressed, and he was afflicted, yet
he opened not his mouth* (Isaiah 53:7). *But Jesus remained
silent* (Matthew 26:63).

It can be so easy to yield to temptation and manipulation
because of our own impatience, especially, if like Joseph,
we are innocent. Discovering and following God's plan for
our lives will always call for our patience, trust and
submission. Thomas Manton comments: 'Cheerful patience
is a holy art and skill, which a man learns from God.' *Be*

53

patient, therefore brothers ... See how the farmer waits for the precious fruit of the earth (James 5:7).

God is not haphazard in his dealings with men. He has everything planned to the last detail. Although we rarely see too far ahead, God, our heavenly Father, leads us just one step at a time, graciously unfolding his purpose for our lives (cf Job 23:10). It is the way of faith, with seemingly countless turns and obstacles; many dark periods and difficult terrain, together with times of joy and blessing. The apostle Paul writes in Romans 8:28, *And we know that for those who love God all things work together for good, for those who are called according to his purpose.* This was to be Joseph's experience.

Between the Old and New Testament we have a period of 400 years called the 'Intertestamental Period' (between testaments). During that period, no prophet's voice was heard, no miracles and no record of communication from God. Yet it was at the closure of that period that Christ was born. The apostle Paul reminds us that it was all according to God's timescale. *But when the fullness of time had come, God sent forth his Son ...* (Galatians 4:4). Solomon describes the perfection of God's timing with these words: *He has made everything beautiful in its time.* The birth, death, resurrection and personal return of Christ are all in accordance with his timescale. God's wonderful purpose for Joseph was just a small part of the overall purpose of the Almighty. Bearing in mind the unparalleled greatness and majesty of our glorious God; is it not quite astonishing, that God should take such a personal interest in the everyday detail of the lives of his children? (cf. Psalm 139:1-6).

Although Joseph may have struggled to make sense of all that was happening to him, God was in control and Joseph would soon see the hand of God intervening, bringing about a situation that could only come from God. He may have felt that he had missed his chance for freedom, but not so, he was God's man in waiting. King David also struggled with similar thoughts, he writes: *How long, O Lord? Will you forget me forever? How long will you hide your face from me?* (Psalm 13:1). As we work out the purpose of God in our lives, there may be occasions when we are anxious as we wait for God to answer our prayers. It might be praying for loved ones or friends, or maybe seeking guidance and direction for the future - it could also be our struggle with illness - the reasons are endless!

It is not always easy to persevere and endure under trial, difficulty or uncertainty, but in doing so, Scripture reminds us that 'enduring is character building'. God is doing something with us that is sanctifying and maturing. *Endurance produces character, and character produces hope* ... (Romans 5:4). Sometimes we fret with the passing of a few days or weeks; in Joseph's case, however, thirteen years would elapse between his abduction and exaltation. When his release from prison came at the end of two years, it would have come as a welcome surprise, for Joseph was oblivious to what God was doing in Pharaoh's life behind the scenes.

How are we to know when God's time has come in any given situation? How do we know when to wait instead of taking the initiative? I suggest two possibilities.

Firstly, when we wholeheartedly want only what God wants. This will always be a challenge, yet it brings about the ruling peace of God in our heart. When a person only wants what God wants - they have patience to wait until the will of God stares them in the face - or to put it another way; until it becomes obvious. This often involves coming to an end of ourselves, so that personal ambition ceases to exist. The apostle Paul expressed this with great clarity in Philippians 1:21, *For me to live is Christ, and to die is gain.* The purpose of God in his life was all that mattered, even through hard and difficult times. As the Lord Jesus suffered in deep agony of soul in the garden of Gethsemane, beyond what can be humanly understood, his closing words were in submission to his Father's will: *My Father, if it is possible, let this cup pass from me; nevertheless, not my will, but as you will* (Matthew 26:39b). This was not easy for our blessed Saviour; should it then be any easier for us?

The very essence of coming to faith in Christ involves submitting to the purpose of God - declaring our wholehearted allegiance to him. It is impossible to improve on God's will for our lives. The reason for this is found in Psalm 18:30, *This God-his way is perfect.*

Joseph was ambitious, he wanted to make progress. In itself there is nothing wrong with this, but in Joseph's case it was a disadvantage to try and initiate his own release. God did not want Joseph exalted in this way. When God's time was right he would exalt Joseph, higher than even his dreams would have allowed. During this two year period the Master sculptor was chipping away and re-shaping Joseph for a position of true greatness. The time would come when Joseph would be ready. Without a doubt, we have to assume that Joseph had many inner struggles and his patience severely tested. Remember; we know the story, Joseph didn't!

Secondly, when God moves into action without our involvement. With the passing of *two whole years* who would ever have believed that the first move would come from Pharaoh? Pharaoh had a dream. The fact that this period of time is described *two 'whole' years*, is perhaps an indication that it did not pass quickly and was wearying and difficult for Joseph. It was a long two years. However, we must never underestimate what God can do when we are prepared to wait, even when it stretches us to our limit.

Joseph was thinking only of himself, but God had much more

in mind, including Pharaoh and a wider picture of which Joseph was just a part. Sometime later Joseph would understand this. This comes across in Genesis 50:20 where he seeks to reassure his brothers who were afraid of him, thinking Joseph was out for revenge. Joseph said, *As for you, you meant evil against me, but God meant it for good.* By that time Joseph could see a much larger picture.

Imagine that moment when without any warning Joseph heard the thrust of the keys in the cell door – and the pathway of exaltation had begun! It was now time for the forgotten man to begin the next stage of spiritual education. When a cake is taken out of the oven before its time, it is only half baked - and is fit neither for displaying or eating. In Hosea 7:8 the spiritual condition of Ephraim is described in this way, *Ephraim is a cake not turned.* May God help us to know the blessing of waiting upon him. If you are presently engaged in a struggle, for whatever reason, and you find it difficult to wait upon God, then here are three things to keep in mind.

- God's way is the wisest - even though it doesn't seem that way at times. Our rationale is too small and often in conflict with God.
- God's timing is best. The pressure of this world often creates a distortion with God's way - if we allow it. Sometimes we insist on our own way because we think it's the only way.
- God's grace is sufficient. Whatever our circumstances, there will always be an endless supply of his grace, holding and sustaining where necessary. When the apostle Paul prayed for healing, rather than being healed, God's word to him was, *My grace is sufficient for you, for my power is made perfect in weakness* (2 Corinthians 12:9).

CHAPTER 7

Summoned by the king

Genesis 41:1-16

*Pharaoh dreamed that he was standing by the Nile,
2 and behold, there came up out of the Nile seven
cows attractive and plump, and they fed in the reed
grass. 3 And behold, seven other cows, ugly and
thin, came up out of the Nile after them, and stood
by the other cows on the bank of the Nile. 4 And
the ugly, thin cows ate up the seven attractive,
plump cows. And Pharaoh awoke. 5 And he fell
asleep and dreamed a second time. And behold,
seven ears of grain, plump and good, were growing
on one stalk. 6 And behold, after them sprouted
seven ears, thin and blighted by the east wind. 7
And the thin ears swallowed up the seven plump,
full ears. And Pharaoh awoke, and behold, it was
a dream. 8 So in the morning his spirit was troubled,
and he sent and called for all the magicians of Egypt
and all its wise men. Pharaoh told them his dreams,
but there was none who could interpret them to
Pharaoh.
9 Then the chief cupbearer said to Pharaoh, "I
remember my offences today. 10 When Pharaoh
was angry with his servants and put me and the
chief baker in custody in the house of the captain
of the guard, 11 we dreamed on the same night, he
and I, each having a dream with its own*

interpretation. 12 A young Hebrew was there with us, a servant of the captain of the guard. When we told him, he interpreted our dreams to us, giving an interpretation to each man according to his dream. 13 And as he interpreted to us, so it came about. I was restored to my office, and the baker was hanged."

14 Then Pharaoh sent and called Joseph, and they quickly brought him out of the pit. And when he had shaved himself and changed his clothes, he came in before Pharaoh. 15 And Pharaoh said to Joseph, "I have had a dream, and there is no one who can interpret it. I have heard it said of you that when you hear a dream you can interpret it." 16 Joseph answered Pharaoh, "It is not in me; God will give Pharaoh a favourable answer."

After two whole years, the time had now arrived for a most significant change in Joseph's life. God was about to intervene in such a way that took the initiative out of Joseph's hands. Joseph could do nothing to alter his circumstances; he had tried that and it didn't work. He was oblivious to what was about to take place, yet he was now ready for God to pluck him out of that prison and set in motion the next stage that would eventually lead to his exaltation. In this, we are reminded that we must rest in God's purpose even when we can't see the way ahead or understand what's going on. If we are wholeheartedly committed to the will of God for our lives, and want nothing else, then we can be sure that's what will happen.

Having been with Joseph in the palace of Potiphar and also in prison, God now breaks into Joseph's life by the most unusual means - through a pagan King! Furthermore, he does so in such a way that would be acceptable to Pharaoh and also make sense in the light of the gifts God had given Joseph. We must never underestimate the sovereignty of God, for he is omnipotent and his power and influence are not restricted to the 'Christian' realm alone. We read in Proverbs 21:1: *The king's heart is a stream of water in the hand of the Lord; he turns it wherever he will.* There is nothing in the entire created universe that does not come under God's control. *Have you not known? Have you not heard? The Lord is the everlasting God, the Creator of the ends of the earth ... his understanding is unsearchable* (Isaiah 40:28).

It is God's prerogative to act wherever and whenever he chooses. Right out of the blue God now places his sovereign hand upon Pharaoh. Even the most powerful men in the world have their troubles and Pharaoh was no exception. In this case he had two dreams which proved to be the source of great anxiety. *So in the morning his mind was troubled ...* (verse 8). His response, which would have been his normal practice, was to call the very best of all the magicians and wise men of Egypt. Dreams and their interpretation were common in those days, and so great men such as Pharaoh would have had the most gifted available to him.

As we consider Pharaoh, we must remember that at that time he would have been the most powerful and unreachable man of his day. Yet, as we shall discover, he was not outwith the reach of God. At this time, Egypt was a symbol of unparalleled greatness in the world. It was the centre of culture and learning among ancient civilizations. On this occasion he discovered that none of his magicians or wise men could offer any interpretation to his dreams (verses 1-7). He hired the best and wisest that money could buy, yet without any success.

What Pharaoh didn't understand, was, that it was God who was behind his dreams - this was a new experience, probably the first! Pharaoh's own resources, therefore, proved to be inadequate to bring about a true interpretation. *The natural person does not accept the things of the Spirit of God, for*

*they are folly to him, and he is not able to understand them
because they are spiritually discerned* (1 Corinthians 2:14).

Bearing in mind that Pharaoh would have known nothing
about Joseph or his circumstances - for there was no need;
the most unbelievable thing was about to happen! Pharaoh
would summon the assistance of a Hebrew slave. Had the
cupbearer spoken on Joseph's behalf at the time of his
restoration to his former position as Pharaoh's cupbearer,
the best that Joseph could have expected, was probably being
'released' from prison. However, the time was now right for
Joseph to be released; it was also the right moment in
Pharaoh's life for this encounter - God's timing was perfect;
right to the minute detail! God's purpose was greater than
either of them could have understood; and so through divine
intervention they are brought together.

Once more we see the value and blessing of trusting in the
providence of God: with patience. It is not always necessary
to understand all the circumstances surrounding our lives
(though we would like to) - the important thing is to walk
with the Lord and live in the Spirit, and with sensitivity to his
guiding hand. God's servant Job could say: *Though he slay
me, I will hope in him ...* (Job 13:15). What is Job saying?
'Even if circumstances should lead to my death, then I will
still trust in God'.

The time came when the cupbearer remembered his
experience in prison with Joseph, and how Joseph had
interpreted his and the baker's dreams with perfect accuracy
(verse 9ff). The cupbearer went on to relate to Pharaoh all
that had taken place. Pharaoh immediately sent for Joseph.
This troubled man needed help, even if that meant sending
for a Hebrew slave from prison. This must have been
humbling for Pharaoh - but he was desperate!

Can you imagine the scene when the jailer turned the key

and said to Joseph, come on, get washed, shaved and dressed; Pharaoh wants to see you? He was about to be catapulted into the presence of a pagan King. Just as the Lord had been with Joseph in prison, so now he orchestrates this event. There was no human manipulation or self-will enforced, God was at work!

Joseph's heart must have burned within him and his spirit leapt for joy - God had not forgotten him! How rewarding it is when we see God at work without our meddling; when we see God take the initiative. From a position of seeming hopelessness, despair and the uncertainty of prison life, God stepped in after thirteen years. Joseph would never have chosen this way, yet it was the God-given way of the making of the man. The Psalmist puts it this way: *he had sent a man ahead of them, Joseph, who was sold as a slave. His feet were hurt in fetters; his neck was put in a collar of iron; until what he had said came to pass* (Psalm 105:17-19). Many lessons would have been learned during those years that would have been impossible during a life of ease and plenty. Restrictions, deprivation and the harsh reality of day to day prison life were to be the means of shaping Joseph's life.

F B Meyer comments: 'As a boy, Joseph's character tended to softness. He was spoiled by his father. He was too proud of his coat. He was given to tell tales. He was too full of his dreams and foreshadowed greatness. None of these were great faults, although he lacked strength, grip, and power to rule. But what a difference his imprisonment made in him! From that moment he carried himself with wisdom, modesty, courage, and manly resolution; that never failed him. He acts as a born ruler of men. He carried an alien country through the stress of a great famine, without a symptom of revolt. He holds his own with the proudest aristocracy of the time. He promotes the most radical changes. He learned to hold his peace and wait. Surely the iron had entered his soul!'

Pharaoh demonstrates his spiritual poverty; he is now ready to listen because he has come to the end of himself. This is an important principle for all who would follow Christ and seek to walk according to God's purpose. Jesus said: *If anyone would come after me, let him deny himself and take up his cross and follow me* (Mark 8:34). This principle is also seen in the story of the prodigal son. After approaching his father for his share of the inheritance, he left home and set out to pursue his own dreams and do his own thing. In the process, he exhausted all his resources and his dreams became nightmares. There came a time when he reassessed his position. His thoughts are summed up with these words: *But when he came to himself* (Luke 15:17). This was the turning point in his life. Pharaoh is about to discover that his resources are also limited and that he is not in control of his own destiny: he said to Joseph: *I have had a dream, and there is no-one who can interpret it. I have heard it said of you that when you hear a dream you can interpret it* (verse 15).

We now come to a wonderful moment in Joseph's life; in a sense, Pharaoh lays down the gauntlet. What will Joseph do? He now has the opportunity to exalt himself. How will Joseph respond? Will he spread his feathers before Pharaoh and show him how gifted he is? Will he even use this opportunity to raise his past injustice and innocence? His response will tell us whether or not he has changed. How glorious are the words Joseph now utters! *It is not in me; God will give Pharaoh a favourable answer* (verse 16). Joseph had come a long way since those days of self exaltation before his parents and brothers. The New International Version helps us to understand just how emphatic and clear Joseph's response was: *I cannot do it ...but God will give Pharaoh the answer he desires.* How God longed to hear those words from Joseph! The hand of God had been upon him, reshaping and moulding his character and personality until he was ready for this defining moment.

Perhaps there are situations in our lives where we need to follow the example of the new Joseph. The apostle Paul discovered the value of personal weakness and humility: *My grace is sufficient for you, for my power is made perfect in weakness ... For when I am weak, then I am strong* (2 Corinthians 12:9-10). What a tremendous thing it is when we are brought to the place where we have confidence to leave everything to God; when we can be content and accepting of any and every situation because we have left it in God's hands.

In Romans 12:1-2 the apostle Paul urges the Christians at Rome to surrender completely to the transforming work of God's Spirit and to do this as *living sacrifices.* In so doing, the Christian is able to discern and prove the value of God's will for them, that it *is good and acceptable and perfect* (verse 2). Later in Joseph's life he was able to look back and see how God's great purpose had fallen into place. He was to see a wider picture that involved the birth of a nation and the development of the people of God, through whom Christ the Messiah would come.

As Joseph lay in that pit of despair many years before, he could never have dreamt what was in store for him; he could see no further than his own miserable situation. God took him on a sanctifying journey that he would never have chosen; he could not possibly have understood the vital importance and the long term significance of the changes necessary in his life; and of the implications outwith his own life. The blessings that would follow would be universal in their scope.

You and I may never fully understand how important it is to faithfully walk with God; keep in step with the Spirit and sensitively listen to our Lord, moment by moment and day by day. Yet even the seemingly small or insignificant things to us, may have value and influence beyond which we can ever know in the wider purpose of God. Ours is the way of faith and trust; often 'not knowing' what lies ahead. We read regarding Abraham: *And he went out not knowing where he was going* (Hebrews 11:8). The apostle Paul writes: ... *no eye has seen, nor ear heard, nor the heart of man imagined, what God has prepared for those who love him* (1 Corinthians 2:9).

CHAPTER 8

Can we find a man like this?

Genesis 41:17-38

17 Then Pharaoh said to Joseph, "Behold, in my dream I was standing on the banks of the Nile. 18 Seven cows, plump and attractive, came up out of the Nile and fed in the reed grass. 19 Seven other cows came up after them, poor and very ugly and thin, such as I had never seen in all the land of Egypt. 20 And the thin, ugly cows ate up the first seven plump cows, 21 but when they had eaten them no one would have known that they had eaten them, for they were still as ugly as at the beginning. Then I awoke. 22 I also saw in my dream seven ears growing on one stalk, full and good. 23 Seven ears, withered, thin, and blighted by the east wind, sprouted after them, 24 and the thin ears swallowed up the seven good ears. And I told it to the magicians, but there was no one who could explain it to me."
25 Then Joseph said to Pharaoh, "The dreams of Pharaoh are one; God has revealed to Pharaoh what he is about to do. 26 The seven good cows are seven years, and the seven good ears are seven years; the dreams are one. 27 The seven lean and ugly cows that came up after them are seven years, and the seven empty ears blighted by the east wind are also seven years of famine. 28 It is as I told Pharaoh; God has shown to Pharaoh what he is about to do.

29 There will come seven years of great plenty throughout all the land of Egypt, 30 but after them there will arise seven years of famine, and all the plenty will be forgotten in the land of Egypt. The famine will consume the land, 31 and the plenty will be unknown in the land by reason of the famine that will follow, for it will be very severe. 32 And the doubling of Pharaoh's dream means that the thing is fixed by God, and God will shortly bring it about.

33 Now therefore let Pharaoh select a discerning and wise man, and set him over the land of Egypt. 34 Let Pharaoh proceed to appoint overseers over the land and take one-fifth of the produce of the land of Egypt during the seven plentiful years. 35 And let them gather all the food of these good years that are coming and store up grain under the authority of Pharaoh for food in the cities, and let them keep it. 36 That food shall be a reserve for the land against the seven years of famine that are to occur in the land of Egypt, so that the land may not perish through the famine."

37 This proposal pleased Pharaoh and all his servants. 38 And Pharaoh said to his servants, "Can we find a man like this, in whom is the Spirit of God?"

Last time we left Joseph in a state of readiness, all cleaned up with somewhere to go! The hand of God had reached out to Pharaoh, creating a situation that he himself was unable to resolve. So this man, the King of Egypt and probably the most powerful man in the world at that time; had to call for the aid of one of his own prisoners, Joseph, a Hebrew slave. The Monarch now meets the slave!

Pharaoh revealed the content of his dreams to Joseph. In a few words, the dreams pointed towards seven years of abundant harvests throughout the land, followed by seven years of severe famine. The overall period would be fourteen years. There are two things in particular to note from Joseph's response to Pharaoh.

Firstly: *God has revealed to Pharaoh what he is about to do* (verse 25). Once again Joseph points, not to himself - but to God. He sought no credit or approval; there was no self-seeking or attempt to exalt himself. He directed Pharaoh to God merely as the instrument of God's revelation. Here we have a wonderful picture of a pagan King coming under the direction of God. God can and does speak to the ungodly to fulfil his sovereign purpose. After all, this is the nature of conversion (cf Romans 5:6-11). We cannot tell at this point whether Pharaoh became a believer or not - but he did accept Joseph's counsel, as a man *in whom is the Spirit of God* (verse 38). God began his work in Pharaoh by firstly giving him a troubled mind due to the dreams. Although Joseph had no background or anything to give him credibility (indeed, quite the opposite), Pharaoh must have discerned something about Joseph that was trustworthy and just; something righteous, something godly. God was at work!

Secondly: the reason there were two dreams, both carrying the same meaning, was because 'God had decided'. This was an affirmation of the purpose of God. In general conversation we often repeat what we've just said in order to affirm it, leaving no room for doubt. The double dream meant that nothing would be left to chance; this was something *fixed by God, and God will shortly bring it about'* (verse 32). Detail such as the two dreams with the same interpretation would have carried tremendous significance for Pharaoh. It would help him to understand the vital importance of what was about to happen, and that the very survival of his own nation and indeed the surrounding nations was at stake. This was no small matter. The implications of his response would be far-reaching, beyond even what he could understand.

At this point we must remember who is speaking to Pharaoh and offering him advice - the ex-prisoner, Joseph. As Joseph suggests to Pharaoh what kind of preparations should be made for the future, he also describes the type of person suitable for such a responsibility. It seems clear that Joseph spoke with a calm authority in spite of his present status (or lack of it). Both the interpretation and Joseph's advice to follow, demonstrate that the Spirit of God was at work and that Pharaoh had discerned this. Joseph had already made it clear that God was the author and interpreter of the dreams; there is no reason, therefore, to think that Joseph is either promoting himself or suggesting that he is the man for the job. He had already said 'I cannot, but God can.' Joseph demonstrates by his own example, a principle for all Christians, that is; the pathway to blessing and spiritual maturity is found in true humility and with a spirit of servanthood. Self exaltation only promotes 'self'. Genuine humility keeps 'self out of sight', and so far as the Christian is concerned, it reveals more of Christ.

What a remarkable situation! *This proposal pleased Pharaoh and all his servants.* There was not one dissenting voice! Nothing short of miraculous! Among all Pharaoh's wisest men and government officials under his authority; all those whose counsel would be sought daily: none were in disagreement, not even one! Notice Pharaoh's next question which was addressed to his servants. *Can we find a man like this, in whom is the Spirit of God?* What a question for a pagan King to ask his servants? Pharaoh then answered his own question by saying to Joseph, *Since God has shown you all this, there is none so discerning and wise as you.* God made it known to Pharaoh immediately; there was no waiting period or time for reflection. No conferring with his officials. In all the years of Pharaoh's experience, wisdom and learning as King of

Egypt, he had never been in this position before - but he knew this was the right course of action to take and that Joseph was the man for the job. God had made it known to him. Pharaoh had discerned that Joseph was much more than just a 'wise man', but that in him 'was the Spirit of God'.

Now we can see why God was working away in Joseph's life for thirteen years, preparing him for just such a time as this. He was God's chosen man for this special moment in history. But not only was Joseph God's chosen man, God was also doing something in Pharaoh's life. Pharaoh responds to his situation by actually looking for a man of God! First time ever! Let us never doubt the sovereign power of God; for there is nothing outwith his power or control. He is the Creator and sustainer of this glorious universe and every form of life.

At times, when perhaps we think our problems or situations are beyond us, when we feel at a dead end or have nowhere to turn - then remember this story! The God who intervened in such a miraculous and almost breath-taking way, breaking into a pagan Kings life, is the very same God of all those who believe. We do well to remember these words: 'I cannot, but God can'.

In tracing back the circumstances of Joseph's life, there is one thing that marked him out more than anything else. In spite of his early youthful pride and lack of spiritual maturity - his 'constant companion' was God! Notice the following references to God or the Lord.

- In Potiphar's household: *The Lord was with Joseph ... How then can I do this great wickedness and sin against God* (39:2. 39:9).
- In prison: *The Lord was with Joseph ... Do not interpretations belong to God* (39:21. 40:8).
- Before Pharaoh: *It is not in me, God will give Pharaoh a favourable answer ... God has shown to Pharaoh ... the*

thing is fixed by God, and God will shortly bring it about (41:16. 41:28. 41:32).
- As Prime Minister: *God has made me forget all my hardships ... God has made me fruitful* (41:51. 41:52).

Joseph's story thus far, is a glorious illustration of what God can do with any believer; even you or me. It is also a challenge to walk in fellowship with God and to learn to wait upon him, especially when the road is tough and the way uncertain. How remarkable then, that in human terms, when life seemed hard and cruel, that Joseph was firmly in the hands of his Lord. The reality of this may have been difficult for him to grasp - yet nothing could alter the fact that 'the Lord was with him'. How wonderful it was for Pharaoh to say: *Can we find a man like this?* (41:38). The presence of God was visible in Joseph's ways and words. Surely nothing is more striking and no greater compliment paid than a person being marked out by the visible presence of God in their life. The promise of God's presence is for every child of God and comes from the lips of our Saviour: *I am with you always, to the end of the age* (Matthew 28:20).

When the apostles Peter and John stood before the Jewish council they were astonished at their boldness and authority because they were uneducated men. We read: *And they recognized that they had been with Jesus* (Acts 4:13). Is this not the responsibility of all who follow Jesus Christ as their Lord and Master? Men and women may deny or disagree with what Christians have to say - but they cannot argue with a transformed life: giving off the aroma or fragrance of Christ. *For we are the aroma of Christ to God among those who are perishing ...* (2 Corinthians 2:15). Dare we ask the question - 'Can we find such a person today?'

Amidst this godless age and irreverent world, God looks for men and women who are being transformed into the image of his Son, being changed from one degree of glory to another by his Spirit. He looks for his children to be salt and light. Jesus said: *You are the salt of the earth ... You are the light of the world* (Matthew 5:13-14). The world around us needs men and women just like Joseph, in whom is the Spirit of God.

The future influence of Joseph's life would be far reaching, indeed, throughout the known world at that time. We are now able to witness the blessing that followed a long apprenticeship in the obscurity of an Egyptian prison. It was not where Joseph wanted to be, but it was God's purpose for him; and that's what really matters! Being where God wants you to be at any given time is the all-important thing. Joseph thought nothing was happening during those dark, dismal and testing years - but God was busy! He was purifying and reshaping him to be the kind of man that now stood before Pharaoh. Perhaps the words of Job sum up how Joseph may have felt: *My days are passed; my plans are broken off ...* (Job 17:11). We'll never know what Joseph was thinking during those thirteen excruciating years when his faith was probably tested to the limit. Yet the outcome tells us that he was a man in submission to God's purpose, not knowing what lay ahead. In a very real sense he was like Abraham, for we read regarding him in Hebrews 11:8, *By faith Abraham obeyed ... not knowing where he was to go.*

Is it not true, that too often we gauge our success, spirituality and even our happiness on our circumstances? Although we know that this is not right - perhaps it is often our experience! Like Joseph, when the winds of adversity blow and our circumstances are unfavourable, let us keep trusting; keep believing and *let us run with endurance the race set before us, looking unto Jesus, the founder and perfecter of our faith, who for the joy that was set before him endured the cross ...* (Hebrews 12:1-2).

From Joseph's life comes a great encouragement. Bearing

in mind all that he had gone through - blessing and glory would shoot forth as a snowdrop bursting through the hard winter grounds. Indeed, a harvest of righteousness would eventually follow him.

CHAPTER 9

From Prison to Palace

Genesis 41:39-57

39 Then Pharaoh said to Joseph, "Since God has shown you all this, there is none so discerning and wise as you are. 40 You shall be over my house, and all my people shall order themselves as you command. Only as regards the throne will I be greater than you." 41 And Pharaoh said to Joseph, "See, I have set you over all the land of Egypt." 42 Then Pharaoh took his signet ring from his hand and put it on Joseph's hand, and clothed him in garments of fine linen and put a gold chain about his neck. 43 And he made him ride in his second chariot. And they called out before him, "Bow the knee!" Thus he set him over all the land of Egypt. 44 Moreover, Pharaoh said to Joseph, "I am Pharaoh, and without your consent no one shall lift up hand or foot in all the land of Egypt." 45 And Pharaoh called Joseph's name Zaphenath-paneah. And he gave him in marriage Asenath, the daughter of Potiphera priest of On. So Joseph went out over the land of Egypt.

46 Joseph was thirty years old when he entered the service of Pharaoh king of Egypt. And Joseph went out from the presence of Pharaoh and went through all the land of Egypt. 47 During the seven plentiful years the earth produced abundantly, 48 and he gathered up all the food of these seven years, which occurred in the land of Egypt, and put the food in the cities. He put in every city the food from the fields around it. 49 And Joseph stored up grain in great abundance, like the sand of the sea, until he ceased to measure it, for it could not be measured. 50 Before the year of famine came, two sons were born to Joseph. Asenath, the daughter of Potiphera priest of On, bore them to him. 51 Joseph called the name of the firstborn Manasseh. "For," he said, "God has made me forget all my hardship and all my father's house." 52 The name of the second he called Ephraim, "For God has made me fruitful in the land of my affliction."

53 The seven years of plenty that occurred in the land of Egypt came to an end, 54 and the seven years of famine began to come, as Joseph had said. There was famine in all lands, but in all the land of Egypt there was bread. 55 When all the land of Egypt was famished, the people cried to Pharaoh for bread. Pharaoh said to all the Egyptians, "Go to Joseph. What he says to you, do."

56 So when the famine had spread over all the land, Joseph opened all the storehouses and sold to the Egyptians, for the famine was severe in the land of Egypt. 57 Moreover, all the earth came to Egypt to Joseph to buy grain, because the famine was severe over all the earth.

Compared to the wise men and intelligentsia of all Egypt, Joseph is now declared by Pharaoh to be more discerning and wiser than all: *there is none so discerning and wise as you.*

The instant transformation in Joseph's circumstances is almost beyond belief. Imagine Joseph sitting there in prison, reflecting on past events as he may have done many times; thinking about his parents, remembering his impulsive immaturity and pompous attitude as he flaunted and swaggered around in that coat of many colours. He would also call to mind the darkness and solitude of that horrible pit, his extraction and transportation to Egypt as a slave and sold into the service of Potiphar. Having done well for himself in the household of Potiphar, he is given a position of responsibility because his master saw that the Lord was with him (39:3). Just when things were now looking up for Joseph, his world fell apart once more, for he is falsely accused of raping Potiphar's wife and banished into prison. As he contemplated his future, the only thing he could be sure of was that the Lord would continue to be with him, as he had always been. He had no idea what the next day held other than being the same as the previous day; the same people, the same food, the same prison routine and no indication when, or if, he might ever be released. Then God intervened!

Having been cleaned up and dressed suitable for the occasion, Joseph was transferred from the prison to the palace. There he gave the interpretations that God had given him with regards to Pharaoh's dreams. Now Joseph is exalted by Pharaoh to such a level that even he could never have dreamt. The reward about to be offered to Joseph is that which he had been schooled for during all those years he suffered at the hands of men. Other than his brief attempt to secure his release through the cupbearer (40:14), Joseph had suffered in silence.

The Spirit of God had been at work preparing every fibre of his being; body, soul and mind, for this glorious exaltation. Joseph had been in that sanctifying wheel of adversity and isolation, being reshaped, polished and transformed until this final moment; he is now ready, not perfect - but ready for this momentous occasion which would prove to be the means of survival, not only for the Egyptians, but all other surrounding nations. The forgotten man is about to be exalted! With patience, Joseph had borne his cross, now he is about to wear the crown! Joseph may be viewed here as a type of Christ, for he would be the means of saving countless people. To Egypt and other surrounding nations he was indeed considered a saviour; and just like Jesus, the cross would come before the crown.

Joseph is effectively given the position of Prime Minister. Pharaoh said that only with regard to the throne would he be greater. What telling and wise words come from the lips of the king of Egypt (in conformity with God's purpose): *See, I have set you over all the land of Egypt.* George Lawson (1749-1820) comments: 'It is a sign of great wisdom to be able to give the best counsel, but it is a sign of wisdom also to know good counsel when it is given, and to be ready to follow it.' Pharaoh recognized the wisdom that came from this man of God.

Joseph now faced his most severe test so far. Jesus said: *Whoever exalts himself will be humbled, and whoever humbles himself will be exalted* (Matthew 23:12). He is now exalted and appointed to a position of 'prestige and prosperity'; yet, as already noted, he was ready for it. He neither sought nor craved such a position. Now at thirty years of age, and having been through so much, he seems to be a man at peace with himself and accepting of God's purpose, whatever that might be. There is a sense in which Joseph had come home because it was where God wanted him to be. If there was any ego or self-exaltation still lurking in his heart, it is now banished from his thinking. Home is where God wants you to be - obeying his word and fulfilling his will for your life. Home is when you can genuinely accept all that is happening to you, knowing God's peace and believing *that for those who love God all things work together for good* ... (Romans 8:28).

We must, however, remember that both Pharaoh and Joseph were exercising enormous faith in all that was taking place -

Pharaoh in his complete acceptance of God's word through Joseph, and Joseph believing that the meaning of the dreams would actually take place. We will never know of his inner struggles and the testing of his faith. What would happen if there was no abundant harvest?

The moment of Joseph's installation into his new position has arrived, and so Pharaoh affirms Joseph's new status and responsibility by doing four things.

Firstly, Pharaoh took his own personal signet ring from his hand and put it on Joseph. This ring was also a seal and carried with it the authority given to royal edicts - effectively giving Joseph royal status. He was now to be treated like royalty! When Pharaoh said: *Only as regards the throne will I be greater than you* (verse 40); his intention was not to remind Joseph that he was inferior to himself, but rather, to remind Joseph that he was superior to all other subjects - hence the significance of the ring which came from Pharaoh's own hand. It was quite impossible for Pharaoh to have exalted Joseph any more than he did. Joseph could have gone no higher!

Secondly, although having been washed and dressed in a fitting way to meet Pharaoh, Joseph is now clothed with new attire, that suitable for his new position: royal garments of fine linen; nothing better or more splendid could be found in all Egypt. No longer was it the garment of a prisoner but that of a Prime Minister. All this in just one day! How wonderful our God is! Coats seem to be prominent in Joseph's life. Beginning with the coat of many colours, then in service in Potiphar's house his coat or outer garment is torn from him by Poitiphar's wife. It was then a prisoner's coat which was later exchanged into a respectable coat suitable for his appearance before Pharaoh. Finally, it is a coat or garment that would have surpassed all others in quality and significance; this was truly a coat of honour and exaltation.

If Joseph was not quite ready for his first coat of many colours; he was certainly ready for his new royal robes.

Thirdly, the gold chain was placed around his neck. This was a mark of distinction in keeping with his new status. As with the ring, it was a badge of authority fitting his position.

Fourthly, he is given his own chariot. Looking back over Joseph's life we can see that most of his time was spent under restrictions; as a slave, in service and in prison, but now he is free in the fullest sense, he is at liberty. Pharaoh made Joseph ride in his own chariot, following Pharaoh's state carriage and part of the royal procession. As he rode throughout the whole land he was worshipped and adored by the people who called out before him: *Bow the knee.*

One word describes the outcome of Pharaoh's exaltation of Joseph, it is 'transformation'. In just one day, a day that seemed to be no more than a fleeting moment in time, Joseph's life is completely turned around, a change of environment, a change of clothing, a change of status, a change of direction. The words of the prodigal's father seem fitting when his son returned from a distant country: *Bring quickly the best robe, and put it on him, and put a ring on his hand, and shoes on his feet ... For this my son was dead, and is alive again; he was lost and is found* (Luke 15:23,24). It is as though Joseph was dead but is now alive. Yet we do well to remember that his moment of exaltation would not have come without his years of suffering and isolation - the school of sanctification was the making of the man.

Although one must not stretch the analogy too far, we can see a picture of salvation in Joseph's transformation. The elements are there - from being a slave to being made a son, a child of God. The apostle John writes in 1 John 3:1 *See what kind of love the Father has given to us, that we should be called children of God; and so we are.* From being held in slavehood to sin, to being set free by the power of Christ: *It is for freedom Christ has set us free; stand firm therefore, and do not submit again to a yoke of slavery* (Galatians 5:1).

Then from being clothed with the garments of sinful humanity; in Christ we are clothed with the perfect righteousness of Christ, looked upon as though we had never sinned. *For he has clothed me with the garments of salvation; he has covered me with the robe of righteousness* (Isaiah 61:10). From being in a state of spiritual poverty to receiving *an inheritance that is imperishable, undefiled and unfading, kept in heaven for you* (1 Peter 1:4). As we think on Joseph's new royal status we call to mind what the apostle Paul writes in Romans 8:17, *and if children, then heirs - heirs of God and fellow heirs with Christ.*

The essence of any form of transformation is that it must be visible. This is certainly true in Joseph's case. Bearing a grudge or wanting to get even where a person has been ill-treated is common to life; though not commendable. Although Joseph had been subjected to injustice and ill-treatment throughout his life, especially between age seventeen and thirty, he had no desire to get even.

He did not backtrack to Potiphar's house and seek retribution against him or his wife for falsely accusing him. Having asked the cupbearer to remember him and speak on his behalf in prison, it seems that he had no wish to bring the cupbearer to account because he forgot about him. Later on, when Joseph brings his family through to settle in Egypt, he treated his brothers, not as they deserved, but with love, forgiveness and kindness, holding no bitterness in his heart. He could have brought judgement upon them, but he didn't. Why? Because he was a transformed man and submitted to God's wider purpose. In 50:19 we read of Joseph's response to his brother's plea for forgiveness: *As for you, you meant evil against me, but God meant it for good.*

It is impossible to enter the mind of Pharaoh at this time, yet, that God was at work in his life is perceivable, due to the impact that Joseph had as 'one in whom was the Spirit of God'. That Pharaoh, a pagan king, should in an incredibly short space of time, give Joseph the authority he now possessed to travel throughout the whole land is almost unthinkable - yet absolutely true! What must the Egyptian people have thought when their king demonstrated such a commitment to an unknown man who had been taken from prison? Perhaps the news of Pharaoh's dreams and their interpretation through Joseph had reached their ears. This in turn would have meant that they would see Joseph as one who had their welfare in mind, indeed, as their saviour. Here we have God's man with total liberty and authority over a pagan nation; what a testimony to God's sovereign power and purpose! Is anything too hard for the Lord? Through Joseph, light would shine amidst darkness!

At this time Joseph was thirty years of age and was given a new Egyptian name, Zaphenath-paneah. He was given in marriage to Asenath and later they had two children, Manasseh and Ephraim. The names were important to Joseph. The name Manasseh reminded Joseph that he was able to forget all the hardships of his former days. Likewise Ephraim reminded him that God had made him fruitful in the land of his affliction (41:51-52).

True to God's revelation through Joseph, seven years of plenty followed, indeed, more than plenty, for we are told that *Joseph stored up grain in great abundance, like the sand of the sea, until he ceased to measure it, for it could not be measured* (41:49). God doesn't deal with half measures, the seven years of abundance remind us of the blessings and riches which he bestows on all those who truly love him and are called according to his purpose. *Blessed be the God and Father of our Lord Jesus Christ, who has blessed us in Christ with every spiritual blessing in the heavenly places* (Ephesians 1:3).

The seven years of abundance came to an end as expected, with all the storehouses throughout the whole land full to overflowing. Then the seven years of famine began just as Joseph had said. At this point we are told that all the land of Egypt was famished and the people cried out for bread. The times of super abundance were now to become a distant memory; wonderful at the time but easily forgotten when they are not there. Seven years earlier had Pharaoh not accepted Joseph's interpretation and wise counsel the whole land would now be facing devastation and hunger to the point of death. Pharaoh listened to his people's cry and said, go to Joseph! *What he says to you, do.*

In this we are surely reminded of the words of Jesus' mother at the wedding in Cana of Galilee where she pointed to Jesus to intervene and perform the first recorded miracle in the Gospels. Wine was important at weddings. To the Jewish rabbi wine was symbolic of joy. It was, therefore, a terrible thing and something of an embarrassment for wine to run out at Jewish weddings, as it did here. On this occasion Jesus' mother came to him informing him that there was no wine left. She said to the servants, 'Do whatever he tells you'. At Jesus' command six large stone water jars were filled with water and following his word to draw from the jars, they discovered that not only was there an abundance of water turned into wine, but that the quality of the wine far excelled what they had already tasted (John 2:1-10).

The severe famine now spread throughout the land, indeed, we are told that it had spread over all the earth. Joseph opened all the storehouses which in turn enabled the people to buy grain. Due to Joseph's wisdom and obedience to the purpose of God, many nations would be saved from starvation and death.

CHAPTER 10

God's greater purpose

Genesis 42:1-24

When Jacob learned that there was grain for sale in Egypt, he said to his sons, "Why do you look at one another?" 2 And he said, "Behold, I have heard that there is grain for sale in Egypt. Go down and buy grain for us there, that we may live and not die." 3 So ten of Joseph's brothers went down to buy grain in Egypt. 4 But Jacob did not send Benjamin, Joseph's brother, with his brothers, for he feared that harm might happen to him. 5 Thus the sons of Israel came to buy among the others who came, for the famine was in the land of Canaan.

6 Now Joseph was governor over the land. He was the one who sold to all the people of the land. And Joseph's brothers came and bowed themselves before him with their faces to the ground. 7 Joseph saw his brothers and recognized them, but he treated them like strangers and spoke roughly to them. "Where do you come from?" he said. They said, "From the land of Canaan, to buy food." 8 And Joseph recognized his brothers, but they did not recognize him. 9 And Joseph remembered the dreams that he had dreamed of them. And he said to them, "You are spies; you have come to see the nakedness of the land." 10 They said to him, "No, my lord, your servants have come to buy food. 11

We are all sons of one man. We are honest men. Your servants have never been spies."

12 He said to them, "No, it is the nakedness of the land that you have come to see." 13 And they said, "We, your servants, are twelve brothers, the sons of one man in the land of Canaan, and behold, the youngest is this day with our father, and one is no more." 14 But Joseph said to them, "It is as I said to you. You are spies. 15 By this you shall be tested: by the life of Pharaoh, you shall not go from this place unless your youngest brother comes here. 16 Send one of you, and let him bring your brother, while you remain confined, that your words may be tested, whether there is truth in you. Or else, by the life of Pharaoh, surely you are spies." 17 And he put them all together in custody for three days. 18 On the third day Joseph said to them, "Do this and you will live, for I fear God: 19 if you are honest men, let one of your brothers remain confined where you are in custody, and let the rest go and carry grain for the famine of your households, 20 and bring your youngest brother to me. So your words will be verified, and you shall not die." And they did so. 21 Then they said to one another, "In truth we are guilty concerning our brother, in that we saw the distress of his soul, when he begged us and we did not listen. That is why this distress has come upon us." 22 And Reuben answered them, "Did I not tell you not to sin against the boy? But you did not listen. So now there comes a reckoning for his blood." 23 They did not know that Joseph understood them, for there was an interpreter between them. 24 Then he turned away from them and wept. And he returned to them and spoke to them. And he took Simeon from them and bound him before their eyes.

The story of Joseph began with a family. Until now, we have centred our thoughts on just one person - Joseph. It is now time for Joseph's family to come back into the story. Although Joseph had been groomed and moulded by the Spirit of God for a special purpose and position, which he now occupied, God had an infinitely greater and incredibly far reaching plan. Indeed, it involved the birth and development of a nation, through which, our Lord and Saviour, Jesus Christ, would eventually come.

Before moving on with our story, it is worth remembering that there is a principle here that affects all of God's children. From the day that we came to know Christ personally, we set out on a journey of discovery; discovering more about ourselves, and, more importantly, about our Lord Jesus Christ. As it was with the apostle Paul, this must also be our life's ambition: he said, *Indeed, I count everything as loss because of the surpassing worth of knowing Christ Jesus my Lord* (Philippians 3:8).

Though our journey is very personal, we are only a small part of something much bigger, indeed; something we do not have the insight to grasp. As we seek to live faithfully for Christ, in obedience and love, we shall never understand how important the influence of our lives may be. Our words and our ways should be an open book for all to see; salt and light to the world. Surely most of us can look back and call to mind certain individuals who influenced us for good - people in whom we saw integrity and godliness.

Some of the greatest men and women in Church history: those who left their mark on literature, missionary enterprise and various types of ministries; were first influenced by some very plain and simple people, such as their Sunday school teacher, Bible class leader or Christian friend. Put simply; and like Joseph, we may be oblivious to the greater and wider purpose of God, of which you and I are just a small piece in the jigsaw. Our faithful living for Christ may have an impact in a wider realm than we will ever know.

In 35:11, God had made a promise to Joseph's father, Jacob, which at that time, he would not have understood. *And God said to him, I am God Almighty: be fruitful and multiply. A nation and a company of nations shall come from you, kings shall come from your own body.* As things stood, Jacob's family numbered no more than 70 and they lived in a most hostile environment. They were surrounded by the Canaanites who presented a real threat to their existence. God's plan was now to bring them to Egypt in order to preserve them. Joseph was to play a vital role in all of this. Of course, neither Joseph or Jacob his father knew anything about God's wider purpose at that time.

God was going to raise up a very special people ... called to be holy and set apart from all other heathen nations around them. They would be brought from Canaan, and in due course each son would become the head of each of the twelve tribes which would make up the nation of Israel.

When the years of the famine came, it was not just the land of Egypt that would be   affected. Back in Canaan Joseph's family were also suffering and in great need of grain. Having heard from others who had been to Egypt for grain, Jacob said to his sons: *Behold, I have heard that there is grain for sale in Egypt. Go down and buy grain for us there, that we may live and not die.* In verse 1 however, we find that the very mention of Egypt startled the sons - and no wonder; it must have sent shivers down their spine. What a moment! The very mention of that name would bring their past deeds right to the surface. The fear and horror of the past could be seen in their faces, for Jacob said to them: *Why do you look at one another?*

It's not surprising that this happened, because before they could eventually immigrate to Egypt, God had work to do in their hearts. Their consciences were now being awakened: this was the beginning of a journey that would soon bring them face to face with their past. This had to be; for change had to take place in their lives before they would eventually be ready to fulfil God's purpose for them - which was, to become leaders of their own respective tribes.

God had to bring the brothers to a point where their past sins of 22 years could be dealt with. As is the case with all sin, it is a barrier to fellowship with God; and if left un-dealt with, it will hinder God's purpose in our lives. Unforgiven sin will grieve the Holy Spirit and create a barrier to our relationship with God. God would use these circumstances to bring about reconciliation with Joseph. And so, Jacob sent ten of his sons off to Egypt, leaving the youngest, Benjamin, behind for fear that harm might come to him.

We are not given much information regarding how Joseph administered his responsibilities with regards to the allocation of the grain, yet such was the importance of this, that even as Governor over the land, he personally undertook certain transactions. It is, therefore, not surprising that the first person the brothers faced, was Joseph! Who was the last person they ever wanted to see, Joseph? But that's just what God arranged! More than twenty years had passed since they had ripped his coat of many colours from his back and sold him as a slave into Egypt.

As they stood before Joseph, it was not the face of a tender youth they had once dispatched to Egypt that they saw, but a mature, wise man, robed according to his status as governor of the land. This moment was the fulfilment of Joseph's dreams many years before, the same dreams that had raised up such hatred among them that they had to get rid of him - or so they thought! Now they bow with their faces to the ground, in subjection to him; as they did so they did not recognize him. Time may have passed by and much had happened, but God's purpose for all concerned continued.

When Joseph looked at his brothers, he recognized them - yet he exercised great restraint. We'll never know just how churned up his emotions were inside, it must have been very difficult for him, but he managed to cover up for the time being by treating them harshly. It was probably his way of coping with the situation. Speaking roughly and interrogating them as though they were spies he is able to find out all about them - that his father and other brother were still alive.

Once more, Joseph was faced with a real test! Before him stood those who had treated him with violence, hatred and injustice. Those who were responsible for setting in motion all that had led to his suffering, rejection and loneliness - the very source of all this was now before him; and he was now in the position to do something about it. Furthermore, they had deliberately allowed their father to go through the torture of thinking that Joseph had been killed by a wild animal and enter into grief. What would Joseph do? To what extent had he changed? Had he allowed hatred to build up during his years in prison; did he long for the opportunity to get even? Was vengeance in his mind? No! Joseph had buried the hatchet and carried no grudges. This is how it must be if we are to walk in fellowship with God.

Such thinking may be common to man - but not Joseph! God had done a great and sanctifying work in his life; he was truly 'God's man'. Here was the mark of a man, who, in spite of the cruel ways he had been treated over those years, was able to continue in fellowship with God, and walk according to his ways.

Joseph's experience of triumphing over evil and wrong is a wonderful example for all who seek to follow Christ, for sin need not have the final say. The apostle John says: *Little children, you are from God and have overcome them, for he who is in you is greater than he who is in the world* (1 John 4:4). Joseph's example teaches us that no matter what adversities or difficulties we may face in life, when we stay focused on God and his purpose and rely on his strength; then not only can we be victorious and overcome, but also bring glory to God through our transformed lives.

According to verse 9, Joseph remembered the dreams concerning his brothers. How remarkable this is! He had moved on in the things of God to such an extent that he had all but forgotten those dreams. They were in the distant past - yet they were significant, for they pointed towards this very situation. Those youthful days of self-exaltation were long gone - Joseph had learned to leave things to God. He was able to see the hand of God in all that had happened in the early days. Later in 50:20 Joseph said to his brothers; assuring them of his forgiveness and that he was not seeking retribution: *As for you, you meant evil against me, but God meant it for good, to bring it about that many people should be kept alive, as they are today.*

It must have been difficult for Joseph to be patient with his brothers, when, during their interrogation, they actually said: *We are honest men.* As Joseph continually accused them of being spies (knowing they were not), they were unaware that he could understand them, because he used an interpreter to communicate with them. They didn't know it but he could understand their every word. He saw, listened and heard it all - they had not changed! Honest men! They must be joking!

This whole scenario brought back the times when they dealt badly with Joseph. They could even remember his distress and his plea for mercy and how that they did not listen to him. Reuben also recalled his request for them to let Joseph go. It was of course Reuben, who, 22 years before had suggested leaving Joseph in the pit so that he could sneak back and pull him out; but even that plan failed, for he was sold as a slave. Unforgiven sin does not lessen or disappear with the passing of time - they could remember every detail, it still weighed heavily upon them.

Joseph had the brothers kept in custody for three days and then arranged for Simeon to be kept in Egypt until they returned. And so, they were allowed to return with a supply of food on the condition that they brought the youngest son, Benjamin, back with them. Benjamin was Joseph's blood brother; they both shared the same mother, Rachel. For this reason Benjamin and Joseph were especially close. Knowing that they were in desperate need of grain back in Canaan, he wasted no time in allowing them to return to their father. Before they left he made sure they saw Simeon being bound: *he took Simeon from them and bound him before their eyes* (verse 24).

Joseph had no desire to treat them cruelly but he had to play the part to maintain anonymity. It was also a necessary part of the plan to bring the family to Egypt. In verse 24 we come to a most remarkable scene where Joseph could not keep his emotions in check any more: *Then he turned away from them and wept.* Not vengeance, not hatred, not getting even with them - but tears, tears of love, compassion and forgiveness; his heart went out to them. It was not yet time for them to see his tears so he turned away; that time would come.

It is not possible to read these words without recalling that Jesus also wept. As he stood over Jerusalem and thought on the spiritual poverty and need of his own people, we read that *he wept over it* (Luke 19:41). Furthermore, at the death of his friend Lazarus as an expression of love, we read: *Jesus wept* (John 11:35). Once more Joseph may be seen as a type of Christ. The brothers could easily have been considered by him as enemies because of how they had treated him - but Joseph loved them and was about to become their saviour by making provision not only of food, but also their future development as a nation. He did not treat them as they deserved! (cf Psalm 103:10).

There are many lessons to be learned from the life of Joseph, but there is one that stands out above all others. It is the challenge of growing into the likeness of our Lord Jesus. The sanctifying work of the Holy Spirit in Joseph's life is there for all to see. When he gave the interpretation to Pharaoh's dreams, he pointed towards God, not himself. He sought no credit. Then at his exaltation to become governor of the land and given his own chariot, there was no banner-waving or pompous attitude. The authority given to him over the whole land and over every subject, except Pharaoh himself, did not lead to self-exaltation; indeed, it was the spirit of a servant that marked him out. He carried out all his duties as a faithful witness to his God. Never at any time did he seek to please others or compromise his faith. He was a bright light amidst heathen darkness. The impact of his transformed life is a testimony to what God can do with those; even you and I - who are prepared to honour Christ in every part of our lives.

CHAPTER 11

God orchestrating events

Genesis 42:25-38

25 And Joseph gave orders to fill their bags with grain, and to replace every man's money in his sack, and to give them provisions for the journey. This was done for them. 26 Then they loaded their donkeys with their grain and departed. 27 And as one of them opened his sack to give his donkey fodder at the lodging place, he saw his money in the mouth of his sack. 28 He said to his brothers, "My money has been put back; here it is in the mouth of my sack!" At this their hearts failed them, and they turned trembling to one another, saying, "What is this that God has done to us?"
29 When they came to Jacob their father in the land of Canaan, they told him all that had happened to them, saying, 30 "The man, the lord of the land, spoke roughly to us and took us to be spies of the land. 31 But we said to him, 'We are honest men; we have never been spies. 32 We are twelve brothers, sons of our father. One is no more, and the youngest is this day with our father in the land of Canaan.' 33 Then the man, the lord of the land, said to us, 'By this I shall know that you are honest men: leave one of your brothers with me, and take grain for the famine of your households, and go your way. 34 Bring your youngest brother to me. Then I shall know that you are not spies but honest men,

and I will deliver your brother to you, and you shall trade in the land.'"
35 As they emptied their sacks, behold, every man's bundle of money was in his sack. And when they and their father saw their bundles of money, they were
afraid. 36 And Jacob their father said to them, "You have bereaved me of my children: Joseph is no more, and Simeon is no more, and now you would take Benjamin. All this has come against me." 37 Then Reuben said to his father, "Kill my two sons if I do not bring him back to you. Put him in my hands, and I will bring him back to you." 38 But he said, "My son shall not go down with you, for his brother is dead, and he is the only one left. If harm should happen to him on the journey that you are to make, you would bring down my gray hairs with sorrow to Sheol."

In the previous chapter we left the story of Joseph with the brothers having come face to face with Joseph. Many years had passed and they did not recognize him. Firstly, because of his change in appearance; he was only a teenage boy when they last saw him, and now he is nearly forty. Secondly, because of his status and position they would have considered him to be an Egyptian. Thirdly, he was the last person they ever expected to see again. Joseph recognized them but gave no clue as to his identity; he spoke to them through an interpreter.

Joseph treated them roughly, even accusing them of being spies. This was probably a way of protecting his own emotions, for at one point he had to turn away and weep. Tears, yes, but not a hint of vengeance! No such thought occupied his heart in spite of how his brothers had treated him in former days. Before sending them back to Canaan with their supplies, Joseph had Simeon bound and detained until the others returned with Benjamin, the youngest brother.

Joseph may have been tempted to reveal his true identity to his brothers, but it was not the right time. The greater and mightier purpose of God could have been jeopardised. Had Joseph told his brothers who he was, even offering forgiveness and reassuring them at this stage, it could have driven such fear into them, that on their way home they could easily have thought up some hair-brain scheme to cover their former tracks. No! It was not time to tell them. In this we see Joseph being directed by the Spirit of God in contrast to his natural instinct. Waiting is never easy, yet the best was yet to be for all concerned and the greater glory of God.

And so, as Joseph arranged to have their sacks filled with grain, he put more than just grain into them; for he returned every penny they had paid. He would not profit from his family but deal with them, not as they deserved, but graciously and gratuitously. He could not bear the thought of taking money from his father.

Our God is a great big God, who does the miraculous and the impossible. He is the God of all creation and nothing is outwith his power or control. The prophet Isaiah comments in 40:17-18; 21-23: *All the nations are as nothing before him, they are accounted by him as less than nothing and emptiness. To whom then will you liken God, or what likeness compare with him? Do you not know? Do you not hear? Has it not been told you from the beginning? Have you not understood from the foundations of the earth? It is he who sits above the circle of the earth, and its inhabitants are like grasshoppers; who stretches out the heavens like a curtain, and spreads them like a tent to dwell in; who brings princes to nothing, and makes the rulers of the earth as emptiness.*

In the events before us, it is this same God who is interested, even, in the smallest detail of our lives: how wonderful! As the brothers journeyed home to Canaan, perhaps still perplexed at the treatment received by the governor of the land, they stopped for a break and also to care for the donkeys. One of the brothers opened his sack to give his donkey some grain and is staggered at what he sees: there was his money pouch sitting there, right on top of the grain; it was the first thing he saw. A small detail indeed, yet as he shared this news with his brothers, we read: *their hearts failed them, and they turned trembling to one another, saying, 'What is this that God has done?'*

Their consciences were still raw from their experience in Egypt; their minds had been taken back to the way they had treated the teenage Joseph many years before. They would also go over the way the governor (Joseph) had harshly dealt with them, accusing them of spying and finally having their brother Simeon kept in custody until they returned; this brought all their past guilt before them. Now, to compound matters, why had the money been put back into their sacks? Was this part of a set-up to prove the governors accusation of spying? What was this all about? Not surprisingly, they blame God. *What is this that God has done?* Was God trying to get even with them? Certainly not! This is not how God works. It is quite amazing how prone people are to blame God when faced with adverse circumstances, yet slow to praise him when they are being blessed.

On the plus side, at least they mentioned God; he has now come into their thinking. As they continued on their way home they must have been working out how they could possibly explain to their father all that had happened. Of course they would have to avoid their inner thoughts and fears in relation to Egypt and Joseph. It must have been an anxious journey, trying to make sense of it all in such a way that would be understood by their father Jacob.

Having arrived home safely and with their tale of woe all ready to be told, they met with their father and *told him all that had happened.* Point by point they went over all the detail of how *the lord of the land* (Joseph) had accused them of being spies and treated them harshly. In response to this accusation they went on to tell their father that they pleaded their case as *honest men.* They continued to explain that the *lord of the land* insisted they prove their honesty by leaving Simeon, return home with the supplies and bring back Benjamin, the youngest son, to Egypt. Then he would know that they were telling the truth. Furthermore, the plot deepens when they explained that their money, which was duly paid for the grain, was found in the mouth of their sacks on their way home.

What must Jacob have thought? Many years before he would remember them coming to him with the false tale of Joseph's disappearance, allowing their father to think that he had been killed by a wild animal. Now they come to explain why another brother is not with them, and not only that, they want to take the youngest back to Egypt with them. Jacob must have felt like exploding inside. If anyone knew these sons it was their father. He knew their personalities and characters; he knew their good points and their bad points; he also knew who could be trusted most. Jacob has had enough! He is full of self pity, and rightly so. He says *You have bereaved me of my children: Joseph is no more, and Simeon is no more, and now you take Benjamin. All this has come against me.*

Self pity caused Jacob to overreact, because he spoke as though Simeon was dead and Benjamin heading in the same direction. Why did Jacob arrive at such a conclusion? The only basis for his thinking was their past reputation. Although Jacob held his sons responsible for all this, it is worth bearing in mind, that years before, when Joseph was just a boy, it was Jacob who spoiled Joseph and made him his favourite.

This in turn only gave the other brothers reason to vent their anger against him. Of course Joseph didn't help by flaunting his special coat. There may have been times when Jacob engaged in personal reflection, and looking back, wished he had handled his sons more wisely. Perhaps he felt partly responsible.

Jacob's response to his situation was to say: *Everything is against me.* This was his natural reaction; it was how he felt. This is quite a common expression. With the best will in the world perhaps most of us allow such a thought to pass through our minds at some point or other. George Lawson (1749-1820) commenting on Jacob's response, writes: 'The words before us are the expressions of that peevishness and dejection which are ready to find place in the heart even of a good man in a day of darkness.' Although you could not have told Jacob at that time, everything was not against him, quite the opposite; he just couldn't understand the reason why all these things were happening, nor could he be expected to.

Jacob had no idea what God was orchestrating in the background. He did not understand that in the greater purpose of God, Joseph had to be removed to Egypt many years before. And now to complete this part of the story, Simeon had to be left as a kind of pawn which would soon lead to the removal of the whole family to Egypt. In due course, Benjamin would also be a vital part of this. Step by step God was using Joseph, Simeon and Benjamin to cause Jacob to uproot from Canaan.

We read of Abraham in Hebrews 11:8, *By faith Abraham obeyed when he was called to go out to a place that he was to receive as an inheritance. And he went out, not knowing where he was going.* In many respects this would be true of Jacob; for God was going to create one mighty nation from this one family - a spiritual offspring that would eventually be too numerous to number. The glory of this would be seen in the development of Israel in the Old Testament and then through the New Testament; in particular through the finished work of Christ on the cross. Jacob could never have understood the immensity of all this. Who could?

This is how God often works. As he directs our lives we may be introduced to circumstances and events that we ourselves would not have chosen (just like Jacob), yet they are all part of his sanctifying purpose; all part of a wider picture. In turn, God looks for our continual faith and trust. God calls for our submission to his sovereign purpose without knowing all the details at any given stage. God's servant Job put it this way: *Though he slay me, I will hope in him ...* (Job 13:15).

The thought of Jacob parting with his youngest son Benjamin, is just too much for him. Reuben makes a plea on the basis that if he does not return with Benjamin from Egypt, then Jacob may kill his own two sons. Of course, this is quite illogical; Jacob would never do such a thing for it would only compound his sorrow. However, such is the intensity of the situation and the degree of Reuben's commitment that this was how he expressed himself. Jacob dug in his heels; there was no way he could allow Benjamin to be taken to Egypt. When Jacob said, *My son shall not go down with you, for his brother is dead, and he is the only one left* - he was referring to Joseph, because Joseph was Benjamin's natural brother, both born to Rachel. According to Jacob's understanding at that time, should he part with Benjamin and he did not return, then both his children born to Rachel would be no more. Such a thought, says Jacob, would bring a depth of sorrow that could bring about my death.

CHAPTER 12

Joseph weeps!

Genesis 43:1-34

43 Now the famine was severe in the land. 2 And when they had eaten the grain that they had brought from Egypt, their father said to them, "Go again, buy us a little food." 3 But Judah said to him, "The man solemnly warned us, saying, 'You shall not see my face unless your brother is with you.' 4 If you will send our brother with us, we will go down and buy you food. 5 But if you will not send him, we will not go down, for the man said to us, 'You shall not see my face, unless your brother is with you.'" 6 Israel said, "Why did you treat me so badly as to tell the man that you had another brother?" 7 They replied, "The man questioned us carefully about ourselves and our kindred, saying, 'Is your father still alive? Do you have another brother?' What we told him was in answer to these questions. Could we in any way know that he would say, 'Bring your brother down'?" 8 And Judah said to Israel his father, "Send the boy with me, and we will arise and go, that we may live and not die, both we and you and also our little ones. 9 I will be a pledge of his safety. From my hand you shall require him. If I do not bring him back to you and set him before you, then let me bear the blame forever. 10 If we had not delayed, we would now have returned twice."

11 Then their father Israel said to them, "If it must be so, then do this: take some of the choice fruits of the land in your bags, and carry a present down to the man, a little balm and a little honey, gum, myrrh, pistachio nuts, and almonds. 12 Take double the money with you. Carry back with you the money that was returned in the mouth of your sacks. Perhaps it was an oversight. 13 Take also your brother, and arise, go again to the man. 14 May God Almighty grant you mercy before the man, and may he send back your other brother and Benjamin. And as for me, if I am bereaved of my children, I am bereaved." 15 So the men took this present, and they took double the money with them, and Benjamin. They arose and went down to Egypt and stood before Joseph.

16 When Joseph saw Benjamin with them, he said to the steward of his house, "Bring the men into the house, and slaughter an animal and make ready, for the men are to dine with me at noon." 17 The man did as Joseph told him and brought the men to Joseph's house. 18 And the men were afraid because they were brought to Joseph's house, and they said, "It is because of the money, which was replaced in our sacks the first time, that we are brought in, so that he may assault us and fall upon us to make us servants and seize our donkeys." 19 So they went up to the steward of Joseph's house and spoke with him at the door of the house, 20 and said, "Oh, my lord, we came down the first time to buy food. 21 And when we came to the lodging place we opened our sacks, and there was each man's money in the mouth of his sack, our money in full weight. So we have brought it again with us, 22 and we have brought other money down with us to buy food. We do not know who put our money in our sacks." 23 He replied, "Peace

to you, do not be afraid. Your God and the God of
your father has put treasure in your sacks for you.
I received your money." Then he brought Simeon
out to them. 24 And when the man had brought
the men into Joseph's house and given them water,
and they had washed their feet, and when he had
given their donkeys fodder, 25 they prepared the
present for Joseph's coming at noon, for they heard
that they should eat bread there.

26 When Joseph came home, they brought into the
house to him the present that they had with them
and bowed down to him to the ground. 27 And he
inquired about their welfare and said, "Is your father
well, the old man of whom you spoke? Is he still
alive?" 28 They said, "Your servant our father is
well; he is still alive." And they bowed their heads
and prostrated themselves. 29 And he lifted up his
eyes and saw his brother Benjamin, his mother's
son, and said, "Is this your youngest brother, of
whom you spoke to me? God be gracious to you,
my son!" 30 Then Joseph hurried out, for his
compassion grew warm for his brother, and he
sought a place to weep. And he entered his chamber
and wept there. 31 Then he washed his face and
came out. And controlling himself he said, "Serve
the food." 32 They served him by himself, and them
by themselves, and the Egyptians who ate with
him by themselves, because the Egyptians could
not eat with the Hebrews, for that is an abomination
to the Egyptians. 33 And they sat before him, the
firstborn according to his birthright and the
youngest according to his youth. And the men
looked at one another in amazement. 34 Portions
were taken to them from Joseph's table, but
Benjamin's portion was five times as much as any
of theirs. And they drank and were merry with
him.

Last time we left Jacob feeling that everything was against him (when the opposite was true, he just didn't know it) and refusing to let the brothers go back to Egypt with Benjamin, as Joseph had insisted upon. During this dilemma at the family home in Canaan, back in Egypt, poor Simeon must have wondered what the outcome of all this would be. He would have known just how difficult it would have been for Jacob to part with Benjamin, if at all. Furthermore, how long would he be kept under restraint in Egypt? His own future was uncertain. We must remember that a considerable time had passed since the brothers had returned home, for they had finished all the food they had brought. During that period of severe famine, every bite that they ate must surely have increased their anxiety.

And so Jacob tells his sons to go back and get more grain. He seems oblivious to the fact that they cannot go back without taking Benjamin. Jacob, probably deliberately, has blocked this thought from his mind - he cannot face such a thought. And so Judah reminds him that it's useless to go back without Benjamin. Jacob is struggling to come to terms with this and questions their honesty and openness before Joseph (the governor). He said to them, *why did you ... tell the man that you had another brother?* Neither Jacob or his sons understood what God was doing behind the scenes, in particular, that Joseph was governor in Egypt. We see God at work here, because had the brothers told Joseph a lie about their family - he would have known.

The situation was a very difficult one and not easy to resolve. They are almost starving, and need to get food quickly or they will die. Eventually, following Judah's continual plea with his father, Jacob has no alternative but to give in and allow Benjamin to go with them. As they prepare to return to Egypt, Jacob tells them to take some of the choice fruits from Canaan as a gift for the governor, and also double the money. We have no record of their conversation during the journey, but they must have been anxious and tense. Let us not forget that during this period Joseph must also have had his own thoughts. Would they come back? Could they be trusted? After all, they had abandoned him many years before; could they do the same with Simeon? Anxious times for all concerned.

Their journey came to an end; they arrived in Egypt and are about to present themselves before Joseph. How were the brothers feeling at this point? The one thing they had carried for twenty-two years was their sin against Joseph and their father; they still lived in fear of it. Because they had never been forgiven by Joseph or confessed their sin to Jacob, they remained in bondage. A deep sense of guilt had stayed with them because their sin had never been dealt with - all that was about to change; although they were unaware of it. The words of Psalm 53:5 sums up their situation: *There they are, in great terror, where there is no terror!* Later, in Genesis 45:3 when Joseph revealed his identity to them, we read: *But the brothers could not answer him, for they were dismayed at his presence.* Put simply - they were scared stiff!

When they were brought before Joseph, Joseph fixed his eyes on Benjamin for the first time in twenty-two years. At this point Joseph gave instructions to his steward to make preparations for a meal and have his brothers brought to his house, treating them with dignity. They continue to be in a state of fear; this is seen by their illogical thinking. They actually thought that this fiasco was arranged by Joseph so that he could steal their donkeys and make them slaves. How ridiculous was this? Joseph, the wealthiest man in Egypt, except for Pharaoh, scheming to steal their donkeys! Fear had driven them to such thinking; their minds were in overdrive!

They are so perplexed by all that is going on that they spoke with Joseph's steward, going over all the detail about their innocence and the money left in their sacks. Little did they know that there was no need to justify themselves, the steward knew all about it! How welcoming the reassuring words of the steward must have been - manna to their souls. The words he spoke to them were truly a 'God-send'. He said: *Peace to you, do not be afraid.* That's exactly what they needed to hear; how gracious of the steward! He went on to explain that God, yes, their God, was behind all that had happened. There was a purpose in all of this that would later be revealed to them. How well they understood what the steward was saying to them is uncertain. The gracious and kindly manner in which the steward dealt with Joseph's brothers is a clear indication of Joseph's godly influence on those who served him.

Because of their past sins against Joseph, they not only carried the guilt, but also expected to be punished for it. Their initial understanding was that God would pay them back, that he would get even with them - but they needed to learn that God doesn't need to get even with anyone for their sin. He is a forgiving, merciful and gracious God. The prophet Isaiah writes in 53:4-5, *Surely he has borne our griefs and carried our sorrows ... he was wounded for our transgressions; he was crushed for our iniquities ... upon him was the chastisement that brought us peace....* This prophetic language pointed towards the Lord Jesus Christ who died for our sins. He took our punishment and paid the penalty for our sins; he seeks our faith, not our fear.

The steward brought all the brothers into Joseph's house and made provision for them to get washed and also feed their animals. They prepared themselves, and also the presents they had brought for Joseph - ready to present them when he arrived at noon. How significant it was, then, that when Joseph arrived, they *bowed down to him to the ground;* thereby fulfilling Joseph's dream from his earlier years. Was Joseph tempted to say; 'do you remember my dreams?' We shall never know, perhaps the thought may have crossed his mind! Much had happened since that day: Joseph had matured, not only as a man, but also spiritually; God had been at work in his life, purifying, sanctifying and preparing him for this occasion. God's purpose for Joseph would have been pre-eminent in his thoughts, not a desire to exalt himself over his brothers.

As Joseph enquired about their welfare, asking about their father in particular, they again bow down and prostrate themselves before him. During this time it would seem that Joseph kept his head low, almost without eye-contact because we read in verse 29, *And he lifted up his eyes and saw his brother Benjamin....* This must have been a terribly difficult moment for Joseph to control his emotions; pretending not to know Benjamin and yet asking questions about him, of which he already knew the answers. However, his emotions soon caught up with him; he could no longer restrain himself and hurried off to his private chamber to weep alone. After Joseph controlled himself, he washed and went back into the room where they were about to eat.

Earlier, Joseph had ordered the killing of an animal in preparation for the brothers to dine with him. All was now ready; the lavish provisions were before them; probably such as the brothers had never seen before. Since their first visit to Egypt, some inexplicable things had happened and were now about to continue. As they sat around the table the brothers noticed that the place settings were all arranged according to their ages. They looked at each other in utter amazement; what was all this about? They had no idea how this could be. We are also informed that Benjamin's portions were five times greater than the others. Although this seems excessive in the extreme, it is really just an expression of how Joseph felt about Benjamin - how fond he was of him; his only true blood brother. It would seem that rather than analyze the further 'strange occurrences', the brothers simply joined in the festivities and were happy in doing so.

We are not told what the topic of conversation was around the table as they relaxed together. Joseph, according to Egyptian tradition, although with them, would have been seated at a different table. We may speculate that Joseph would have put forward some very searching questions regarding how things were in Canaan, in particular in relation to his father. In a relaxed and informal manner Joseph would no doubt have received a full update on all that had happened since his absence many years before. With God's help Joseph was able to say nothing about his true identity - the time would soon be upon them when he would make himself known to his brothers, but not yet! How important it is to learn, under God's guidance, that there are times when saying nothing can be the wisest option.

Why was it that Joseph did not seek vengeance at the first opportunity? Why did he not remind them of their past sins and all the hurt and sadness they had caused not only to him, but also to his father? Perhaps the answer is found in his 'tears'. In Joseph's earlier days as he served in Potiphar's house and then when he was in prison, we are told that *the Lord was with Joseph.* Having experienced the Lord's presence in both success and adversity, there is every reason to believe that Joseph continued to worship the Lord and grow in faith during his years as a prisoner. He was now a changed man and ready for this very moment!

So how did Joseph feel as he looked on his brothers? He felt pity for them. Sorrow filled his heart, not a spirit of vengeance. Yes, they had done some terrible things to him; they had sinned gravely, but they were never able to rid themselves of their guilt and fear; right to this very moment it filled their hearts. During those years they had discovered how deeply sin can ruin your life. Yet during those same years, Joseph also made a discovery - it was the depth of God's love! A love that forgives, heals and restores - a love that feels the hurt of others - a love that has no desire to get even - a love that understands how easy it is to fall into sin.

Just like the Lord Jesus, who does not treat us as our sins deserve, so likewise, Joseph did not treat his brothers as their sins deserved. As the Lord Jesus looked over Jerusalem, *he wept over it* (Luke 19:41). He wanted his own people, Israel, to receive his embrace and feel his love, he longed for them to trust in him. Thinking about their waywardness and hard-heartedness he said, *How often I would have gathered your children together as a hen gathered her brood under her wings, and you would not!* (Matthew 23:37).

Just as the Lord Jesus longed for the reconciliation of his people, so, likewise, Joseph now longed for reconciliation with his brothers. As we shall later discover, Joseph had totally forgiven them, and was therefore, able to love them without any hang-ups or grudges. He was full of compassion for them. His tears said it all!

CHAPTER 13

The final test!

Genesis 44:1-34

44 Then he commanded the steward of his house, "Fill the men's sacks with food, as much as they can carry, and put each man's money in the mouth of his sack, 2 and put my cup, the silver cup, in the mouth of the sack of the youngest, with his money for the grain." And he did as Joseph told him.
3 As soon as the morning was light, the men were sent away with their donkeys. 4 They had gone only a short distance from the city. Now Joseph said to his steward, "Up, follow after the men, and when you overtake them, say to them, 'Why have you repaid evil for good? 5 Is it not from this that my lord drinks, and by this that he practices divination? You have done evil in doing this.'"
6 When he overtook them, he spoke to them these words. 7 They said to him, "Why does my lord speak such words as these? Far be it from your servants to do such a thing! 8 Behold, the money that we found in the mouths of our sacks we brought back to you from the land of Canaan. How then could we steal silver or gold from your lord's house? 9 Whichever of your servants is found with it shall die, and we also will be my lord's servants."
10 He said, "Let it be as you say: he who is found with it shall be my servant, and the rest of you shall be innocent." 11 Then each man quickly lowered

his sack to the ground, and each man opened his sack. 12 And he searched, beginning with the eldest and ending with the youngest. And the cup was found in Benjamin's sack. 13 Then they tore their clothes, and every man loaded his donkey, and they returned to the city.

14 When Judah and his brothers came to Joseph's house, he was still there. They fell before him to the ground. 15 Joseph said to them, "What deed is this that you have done? Do you not know that a man like me can indeed practice divination?" 16 And Judah said, "What shall we say to my lord? What shall we speak? Or how can we clear ourselves? God has found out the guilt of your servants; behold, we are my lord's servants, both we and he also in whose hand the cup has been found." 17 But he said, "Far be it from me that I should do so! Only the man in whose hand the cup was found shall be my servant. But as for you, go up in peace to your father." 18 Then Judah went up to him and said, "O my lord, please let your servant speak a word in my lord's ears, and let not your anger burn against your servant, for you are like Pharaoh himself. 19 My lord asked his servants, saying, 'Have you a father, or a brother?' 20 And we said to my lord, 'We have a father, an old man, and a young brother, the child of his old age. His brother is dead, and he alone is left of his mother's children, and his father loves him.' 21 Then you said to your servants, 'Bring him down to me, that I may set my eyes on him.' 22 We said to my lord, 'The boy cannot leave his father, for if he should leave his father, his father would die.' 23 Then you said to your servants, 'Unless your youngest brother comes down with you, you shall not see my face again.'

24 "When we went back to your servant my father,

we told him the words of my lord. 25 And when our father said, 'Go again, buy us a little food,' 26 we said, 'We cannot go down. If our youngest brother goes with us, then we will go down. For we cannot see the man's face unless our youngest brother is with us.' 27 Then your servant my father said to us, 'You know that my wife bore me two sons. 28 One left me, and I said, Surely he has been torn to pieces, and I have never seen him since. 29 If you take this one also from me, and harm happens to him, you will bring down my gray hairs in evil to Sheol.' 30 "Now therefore, as soon as I come to your servant my father, and the boy is not with us, then, as his life is bound up in the boy's life, 31 as soon as he sees that the boy is not with us, he will die, and your servants will bring down the gray hairs of your servant our father with sorrow to Sheol. 32 For your servant became a pledge of safety for the boy to my father, saying, 'If I do not bring him back to you, then I shall bear the blame before my father all my life.' 33 Now therefore, please let your servant remain instead of the boy as a servant to my lord, and let the boy go back with his brothers. 34 For how can I go back to my father if the boy is not with me? I fear to see the evil that would find my father."

At first glance this chapter might seem unnecessary in the life of Joseph - yet we must remember that God had a work to do in the brothers lives before Joseph would reveal his true identity. This part of the narrative brings before us the brother's final test before Joseph presents himself as their long lost brother. Though Joseph was the key figure in God's greater purpose (within the overall narrative), his family and Pharaoh, king of Egypt, were also part of God's great master plan.

The opening verses might seem rather cruel on Joseph's part. It looks as though he is causing his brothers unnecessary agony by putting the money back in their bags, and, in particular, the silver cup in Benjamin's. Why did Joseph arrange to have the money put into their sacks and in addition his silver cup put into Benjamin's sack? What lay behind this? Was he at last going to get even - surely not? Was he playing some kind of game with them - or was he just being cruel?

To answer these questions we must remember that Joseph was a transformed man. Likenesses to our Lord Jesus were now seen in his life. The old Joseph had died! The truth is; what Joseph did was probably the most loving thing he could have done - even though it must have been very painful to do. It is almost a form of discipline and discipline can be an expression of love. *For the Lord disciplines the one he loves, and chastises every son whom he receives* (Hebrews 12:6). Joseph was still not sure how the brothers would respond when the money and the cup were found in their sacks; in a sense, he was taking an enormous risk! This was to be their 'final test'. It was aimed at testing the sincerity of their previous repentance in 42:21, where they said; *In truth we are guilty concerning our brother....*

Joseph needed to know if they had changed, if they were really genuine. Although Joseph would not have understood the full implication of God's wider purpose; the fact was, the brothers, just like Joseph - had to change. He needed to know if their past actions had brought some form of regret and sorrow, or whether they had become sin-hardened.

Unfortunately, it is possible for a Christian to become insensitive to sin, and in so doing become hardened. The apostle Paul refers to this in 1 Timothy 4:2 when he writes of those *whose consciences are seared.* In the sanctifying work of the Holy Spirit, it is possible to resist change and direction as the Spirit reveals it to us; areas in our lives that need to be dealt with. When we resist, God's work and purpose will be hindered in our lives. True repentance ought always to show itself in outward change. Joseph now wanted to see if the brothers had changed! There was only one way to find out - give them the chance to do the same again!

When Joseph had the money put into his brothers sacks and the silver cup put into Benjamin's sack, he did not know how they would respond, yet it was the only way to find out whether or not they would dare to leave Benjamin (the father's favourite) back in Egypt, just as they had done with 'him' many years before. To carry out this final test was painful for all concerned. Their father's words would still be ringing in their ears; *May God Almighty ... send back your other brother and Benjamin*. They knew that the shock of returning without Benjamin could quite possibly lead to their father's death.

Not only did Joseph need to see a change in his brothers, but they themselves needed to seek God's forgiveness and also learn to forgive themselves, deal with their past and move on without carrying guilt. The brothers had a choice; they could let Benjamin be taken back to Egypt with Joseph's stewards or they could all go with him. What would they do? To prove that they had changed they must return with Benjamin to Egypt - and that's exactly what they did! Back in earlier days when they got rid of Joseph, they tore his clothes from him to fabricate their false story, allowing their father to think he had been killed by a wild animal. Now in verse 13 we read of clothes being torn again - this time, 'their own': *Then they tore their clothes*. The tearing of their clothes was an expression of their sorrow and shock at the present circumstances.

There may be times, when we too, just like the brothers, carry guilt because of some past sin and throughout life we drag it behind us because we've never dealt with it. Just as

Joseph would soon demonstrate total forgiveness towards his brothers, so likewise, we have a wonderful Saviour in our Lord Jesus Christ, who is able to totally forgive us when we repent and seek his forgiveness. Because he has dealt with our sin and guilt on the cross, the apostle John was able to write, *If we confess our sins, he is faithful and just to forgive us our sins and to cleanse us from all unrighteousness* (1 John 1:9).

Though we are instructed in Scripture (Romans 6:1-2) not to continue in sin just because we know there is forgiveness; in a way that is difficult for us to understand, God is still able to use our shortcomings for his ultimate purpose. Our faults, sufferings and difficult times are often used by God as a way of purifying and strengthening us; making us more fit for his service and bringing glory to his name. In Romans 8:28 we read: *And we know that for those who love God all things work together for good, for those who are called according to his purpose.* This may have seemed a cruel blow for the brothers, yet God would use it for their eventual good and his glory.

And they returned to the city: what glorious words indeed! They all returned with Benjamin to try and unravel this mystery. Although they had not travelled too far, Joseph must have been on edge, wondering who would come back. Would they all come, or just Benjamin? Can you imagine how he must have felt as he saw them approaching? Notice once again, that they *fell down to the ground* - they must have been terrified! Joseph is mildly coarse with them and lets them think that by means of divination he would get to the truth. It is important to understand that reference to 'divination' is not meant as a pagan concept here, but conveys the idea that 'God would give him the ability to understand what was happening'.

These men were entirely innocent of this crime; once again

they had been 'set up', yet there is no sign of arrogance or self-justification. Listen to their plea: *What shall we say to my Lord? What shall we speak? Or how can we clear ourselves?* They knew that it was a waste of time to attempt justifying themselves. You see, in their hearts, they still believed that the problem lay in what they did to Joseph many years before - until this was dealt with they would never be free from their sense of guilt. If only they knew who stood before them! Twenty two years before they had made their mistake with Joseph, but now, with Benjamin in mind, they did not do the same again.

The passage following from verse 16 has been described by some scholars as 'one of the greatest pieces of literature on human intercession'. Judah, although not the eldest brother, made a wonderful plea from his heart on behalf of his brothers, beginning with, *Oh, my Lord please let your servant speak a word in my Lord's ear, and let not your anger burn against your servant, for you are like Pharaoh himself.* His motive was to move Joseph's heart to show pity. This is the work of an intercessor - someone who pleads on behalf of another. In the fullest and most complete way this is the work of the Lord Jesus Christ. The prophet Isaiah, in 53:12, writes *... yet he bore the sin of many, and makes intercession for the transgressors.* Hebrews 7:25, *Consequently, he is able to save to the uttermost those who draw near to God through him, since he always lives to make intercession for them.*

As we think on the greatest act of 'substitution' in the history of mankind by our blessed Lord, listen to Judah's tender words in verses 32-34 as he continues his plea for pity and mercy on his brother's behalf: *If I do not bring him back to you, then I shall bear the blame ... Now therefore, please let you servant remain instead of the boy as a servant to my Lord, and let the boy go back with his brothers. For how can I go back to my father if the boy is not with me?* At this point Joseph must have found it unbearable. How was he able to control his emotions? He knew how difficult he was making it for them, but it had to be done. It is no surprise that we read in 45:1 *Then Joseph could not control himself before all those who stood by him.*

CHAPTER 14

Joseph identifies himself

Genesis 45:1-15

Then Joseph could not control himself before all those who stood by him. He cried, "Make everyone go out from me." So no one stayed with him when Joseph made himself known to his brothers. 2 And he wept aloud, so that the Egyptians heard it, and the household of Pharaoh heard it. 3 And Joseph said to his brothers, "I am Joseph! Is my father still alive?" But his brothers could not answer him, for they were dismayed at his presence.

4 So Joseph said to his brothers, "Come near to me, please." And they came near. And he said, "I am your brother, Joseph, whom you sold into Egypt. 5 And now do not be distressed or angry with yourselves because you sold me here, for God sent me before you to preserve life. 6 For the famine has been in the land these two years, and there are yet five years in which there will be neither ploughing nor harvest. 7 And God sent me before you to preserve for you a remnant on earth, and to keep alive for you many survivors. 8 So it was not you who sent me here, but God. He has made me a father to Pharaoh, and lord of all his house and ruler over all the land of Egypt. 9 Hurry and go up to my father and say to him, 'Thus says your son Joseph, God has made me lord of all Egypt. Come down to me; do not tarry. 10 You shall dwell in the land of

Goshen, and you shall be near me, you and your children and your children's children, and your flocks, your herds, and all that you have. 11 There I will provide for you, for there are yet five years of famine to come, so that you and your household, and all that you have, do not come to poverty.' 12 And now your eyes see, and the eyes of my brother Benjamin see, that it is my mouth that speaks to you. 13 You must tell my father of all my honour in Egypt, and of all that you have seen. Hurry and bring my father down here." 14 Then he fell upon his brother Benjamin's neck and wept, and Benjamin wept upon his neck. 15 And he kissed all his brothers and wept upon them. After that his brothers talked with him.

Without any shadow of doubt this passage is one of the most moving and soul touching in all Scripture. It is full of emotion and pathos, surely touching even the coldest heart. To read this narrative thoughtfully and remain unmoved is almost unthinkable. The difficulty facing the writer, is to somehow-or-other, unfold this part of the 'Joseph story' in a way that helps us appreciate, even a little, the glory and uniqueness of the occasion.

Earlier in the story, Joseph had to restrain himself, for the time was not right for him to reveal his true identity: *Then he turned away from them and wept* (42:24). Although under enormous inner pressure to tell them who he was, he had to hold back. He was tortured from within. His youthful dreams had now been fulfilled; the brothers had bowed down before him - more than once. Yet Joseph no longer cared; the things that mattered in his youth no longer carried the same importance. Joseph had matured, having spent years of incarceration and injustice; suffering, yet not understanding why. The sanctifying wheel of adversity had been his constant companion; but the Lord was with him, preparing him for the very situation that now faced him. God's greater purpose lay behind all that had happened in both Joseph and his brother's lives, though at any given stage they would not have known it. It would soon make sense to them all, yet take time for the brothers to come to terms with the scale and significance of it all.

Joseph now bursts with emotion! *Then Joseph could not control himself before all those who stood before him. He cried, 'Make everyone go out from me.' So no one stayed with him when Joseph made himself known to his brothers.* Joseph then wept so loudly that the Egyptians heard him - they must have wondered what was going on! Everyone in Pharaoh's house heard about it. What was happening to Joseph? Why was the governor of the land weeping openly? Previously Joseph had spoken to his brothers through an interpreter, but now he is about to speak to them in their own language. This would shock them!

The moment had arrived that we never tire of reading: *And Joseph said to his brothers, 'I am Joseph! Is my father still alive?'* Imagine this, if you will: picture the scene. Joseph's first concern was for his father, not his own glory or position, not self-exaltation, not making his brothers feel bad about themselves. Self was in the distant past. How remarkable that in the same breath of his self-disclosure that he asks after his father. During all those years of separation his father would often have been on his mind. What torture he must have gone through! Surely he had spent many a sleepless night, staring at a prison ceiling and just wondering how his father was. Should Joseph have been asked, 'what do you want more than anything else in this life, what would it be? There can be no doubt that he would have said, 'I want to see my father'. So then, there was only one question on his mind at this time: 'Is my father alive?'

How typical of a heart that has been touched by the grace of

God and experienced the continual presence of the Lord. No hatred, no vengeance, no casting up, no desire for retribution against his brothers - just love and concern. Joseph bears testimony to a life transformed by the Spirit of God. Is it really possible for someone to change so much? Yes it is, but only when we are willing, and then, by the power of God. To understand how Joseph felt is surely beyond us - we can only imagine!

While Joseph is full of unspeakable joy, his brothers were going through quite different emotions. They were terrified! They were speechless, driven to silence and lost for words. Joseph was the last person they ever wanted to see: *His brothers could not answer him.* Their greatest dread had just become a reality! The dreamer stood before them - and it was a nightmare! The brothers stood face to face with the one who could be their judge, jury and executioner. Joseph was the offended party - and they the guilty, but just like the Lord Jesus, he did not treat them as they deserved. And so Joseph said to them: *Come near to me, please.* Is this how you treat someone who almost killed you and then sold you as a slave? Only when the grace of God has swallowed up all the anger and desire for vengeance!

Joseph didn't say; get out of my sight, but rather, 'please come close to me' (Good News Bible). How wonderful! This is the message of the cross. A message of reconciliation: *And you who were once alienated and hostile in mind, doing evil deeds, he has reconciled in his body of flesh by his death, in order to present you holy and blameless and above reproach before him* ...(Colossians 1:21-22). It would not be long before Joseph would present his brothers before Pharaoh, and he would do so, just as though they had never sinned against him. This reminds us that on a day yet to come, the Lord Jesus will present his children before his Father in heaven, just as though they had never sinned.

Joseph

Joseph's response to his brothers is that of intimacy, warmth and friendship; yet it's more than that - it is an expression of 'total forgiveness'. Notice please, that before Joseph told them who he was, he told everyone to get out of the room. This was going to be difficult in the extreme for his brothers, and Joseph knew that, so he did not want anyone to know of their past demeanours. He had no desire to see them squirm in front of others. He had forgiven them without measure. It wasn't that he had just put the past behind him or chosen to forget. No! He had totally forgiven them! This is seen in that he made them feel at ease with themselves. In verse 5 he says: *And now do not be distressed or angry with yourselves because you sold me here, for God sent me before you to preserve life.*

Joseph's actions remind us once again of God's grace towards those who turn to him in saving faith, for we read in Psalm 103:8-10; *The Lord is merciful and gracious, slow to anger and abounding in steadfast love. He will not always chide, nor will he keep his anger forever. He does no deal with us according to our sins, nor repay us according to our iniquities.*

One of the most difficult things to do is to live your life being fully aware of God's sovereign purpose for you all the time. We may, as we should, live in total submission to God's purpose, yet events and circumstances in our day to day lives may vary from blessing and abundance to trial and difficulty; some of these we understand and others make no sense at all, and we struggle with them. No verse of Scripture affirms God's purpose through all the events of life more than Romans 8:28: *And we know that for those who love God all things work together for good, for those who are called according to his purpose.*

This is the point Joseph is making when he said: *God sent me ahead of you.* It is hard to think that God had allowed the brother's to treat Joseph the way they did so many years before, including all the injustice that followed; yet it was all part of his plan to bring about the events now taking place on a world scale. Only now could Joseph make sense of all that had happened: his own mistakes, his father's favouritism, his brother's envy and cruelty, slavery, injustice, being forgotten, Pharaoh's dreams, famine and his brothers coming for food.

All this and more was woven into the fabric of God's purpose. Joseph used one expression to make sense of twenty-two years of agonizing mystery and also help his brothers to be at ease: *So it was not you who sent me here, but God.* Later in 50:20 Joseph had to remind his brothers of this once more: *As for you, you meant evil against me, but God meant it for good, to bring it about that many people should be kept alive, as they are today.*

The story of Joseph, although a wonderful piece of literature and full of intrigue, sentiment and emotion, is also full of lessons that ought to influence our present-day Christian living. Earlier we touched on the subject of 'reconciliation'; now we witness the practical outworking of it. Joseph had already told his brothers not to get distressed or angry with themselves - now he physically puts this into action.

In verses 14-15 we read, *Then he fell upon his brother Benjamin's neck and wept, and Benjamin wept upon his neck. And he kissed all his brothers and wept upon them.* In response to this we are informed that his brothers talked with him. We must allow Joseph a little self indulgence, for in verse 13 he says: *You must tell my father of all my honour in Egypt, and of all that you have seen.* This was not so much pride, as simply wanting his father to be thrilled and pleased with him.

Who could have believed such an outcome after so many

years of separation? But God was at work! Is anything too hard for the Lord? Picture the scene - see their embrace and hear their sobs. Witness the raw emotions of uncertainty, fear and love as this wonderful God-glorifying reunion takes place. Not a dry eye in the house!

What a lesson we have here for believers who are at a distance from their brothers and sisters in Christ. Those who have fallen out and do nothing about it! Surely, if in any measure we appreciate the fact that Christ has reconciled us to himself, we in turn ought to be reconciled to each other. Matthew 5:24: *First be reconciled to your brother.* In Joseph we have an example to follow.

From this glorious passage, what lessons are worthy of our meditation?

- The need to totally forgive others as our Lord Jesus has forgiven us. To offer our forgiveness to others, thereby putting them at ease.
- To learn to submit to God's sovereign purpose - even although we may not be able to understand or make sense of what is happening around us at any given time.
- To make sure that where there has been a breakdown in our relationships with others, that we initiate reconciliation in a most practical way.

CHAPTER 15

A new inheritance

Genesis 45:16-28

16 When the report was heard in Pharaoh's house, "Joseph's brothers have come," it pleased Pharaoh and his servants. 17 And Pharaoh said to Joseph, "Say to your brothers, 'Do this: load your beasts and go back to the land of Canaan, 18 and take your father and your households, and come to me, and I will give you the best of the land of Egypt, and you shall eat the fat of the land.' 19 And you, Joseph, are commanded to say, 'Do this: take wagons from the land of Egypt for your little ones and for your wives, and bring your father, and come. 20 Have no concern for your goods, for the best of all the land of Egypt is yours.'"

21 The sons of Israel did so: and Joseph gave them wagons, according to the command of Pharaoh, and gave them provisions for the journey. 22 To each and all of them he gave a change of clothes, but to Benjamin he gave three hundred shekels of silver and five changes of clothes. 23 To his father he sent as follows: ten donkeys loaded with the good things of Egypt, and ten female donkeys loaded with grain, bread, and provision for his father on the journey. 24 Then he sent his brothers away, and as they departed, he said to them, "Do not quarrel on the way."

25 So they went up out of Egypt and came to the

> *land of Canaan to their father Jacob. 26 And they*
> *told him, "Joseph is still alive, and he is ruler over*
> *all the land of Egypt." And his heart became numb,*
> *for he did not believe them. 27 But when they told*
> *him all the words of Joseph, which he had said to*
> *them, and when he saw the wagons that Joseph*
> *had sent to carry him, the spirit of their father Jacob*
> *revived. 28 And Israel said, "It is enough; Joseph*
> *my son is still alive. I will go and see him before I*
> *die."*

Previously, we considered that glorious meeting where Joseph revealed his true identity to his brothers, and not only so, but he embraced each one and sobbed almost uncontrollably to such an extent that the household of Pharaoh heard the commotion. He expressed in the most practical way that he had totally forgiven them for their past dealings with him. In doing so he also initiated a spirit of reconciliation. The brothers were then sent back to Canaan to tell their father all that happened; and in particular that his son Joseph was still alive.

In Egypt, Joseph was considered to be a kind of saviour (due to his interpretation of Pharaoh's dreams) and only Pharaoh himself would have been held in higher esteem. Joseph was literally the means of life and death to the nation and carried with his position, unquestioning authority. Yet; when news reached Pharaoh that Joseph's brothers had arrived, he immediately, as an expression of joy and gratitude told Joseph what to do regarding his brothers. He wanted them to be treated with every kindness and no expense spared. Notice verses 19-20: *And you, Joseph, are commanded ... for the best of all the land of Egypt will be yours.* In the nicest possible way Pharaoh exerted his authority. In this, we see the hand of God interacting in a pagan king's life to bring Joseph's entire family down to Egypt.

As commanded by Pharaoh, Joseph told his brothers to load up all the new wagons with the provisions and return to Canaan. Pharaoh wanted all Joseph's family to return and settle in Egypt. They were instructed to have no concern for all their present belongings, but to leave them behind, for they would be given the very best that Egypt could provide. Joseph clearly sensed a rightness in Pharaoh's decision and obeyed without questioning. Provision of food, clothing, money and other requirements were given to them. Once again, Benjamin, as an expression of Joseph's special fondness, was given abundantly more than the rest.

The provisions given and promised to Joseph's family remind us of the wonderful inheritance which belongs to believers in Christ. Paul writes in 2 Corinthians 8:9, ... *though he was rich, yet for your sakes he became poor, so that you by his poverty might become rich.* Peter refers to it in these words: *According to his great mercy, he has caused us to be born again to a living hope ... to an inheritance that is imperishable, undefiled, and unfading, kept in heaven for you ...* (1 Peter 1:3-4). Joseph was told by Pharaoh to remind his family not to hang on to their old belongings - everything would be new! *Therefore, if anyone is in Christ, he is a new creation. The old has passed away; behold the new has come. All this is from God ...* (2 Corinthians 5:17-18).The New Testament letters are full of exhortations to put aside the old and live in the reality of the new (Colossians 3:1-17. 1 Peter 1:13-23. Hebrews 10:19-25: 12:1-3).

The true significance of Joseph's earlier words in verse 5 becomes meaningful: *God sent me ahead of you.* We now discover the wider meaning of this twenty-five year scenario! Being sent ahead by God had not meant an easy passage for Joseph, quite the opposite; yet the pathway chosen by God was right for all concerned - to accomplish what he had planned. At this particular time it would lead to the uprooting of Joseph's whole family. An enormous life-changing commitment.

As Joseph waved them off with 'all things new', he said to them, *Do not quarrel on the way.* He knew his brothers - but more than that; he knew they had much to take in; they had just been shocked to the core. So much had happened that it would take time to make sense of it all. Then, of course, how were they going to explain it to their father? Oh to be a fly on the wall during that homeward journey! What would they quarrel about? Would they discuss who was to blame many years before for the way they dealt with Joseph? What exactly would they say to their father? Would they tell the truth?

I believe that as Joseph waved goodbye, he felt sorry for them. He knew they faced a difficult time before their father - yet this was all part of God's sanctifying work in them. They had to come to terms with their past, they had to experience sorrow and repentance for their actions. Joseph had forgiven them, but how would their father respond? The last time they came home with the name Joseph on their lips, it was with a blood-stained coat in their hands and a pack of scheming lies. On this occasion as they mention his name, they are dressed in brand new clothing, money in their purses, new wagons, food and the promise of future wealth. How would they explain all this?

To their credit, their first words to Jacob, their father, were; *Joseph is still alive, and he is ruler over all the land of Egypt.* How did Jacob respond? He *became numb, for he did not believe them.* The word used for 'numb' means, 'fainted or paralysed'. He was silent and motionless. In spite of Jacob being a man of God who had dreams, wrestled with God and received the promises from God, he had a track record as a schemer and now wondered just what they were scheming, he knew them! This was just too good to be true; surely not possible!

Yet perhaps deep in his heart he had hoped and prayed for

many years that some miracle might take place. He may have hoped against all odds. If this was so - then God had answered his prayers. The words of the prodigal son's father are fitting: *For this my son was dead, and is alive again; he was lost and is found* (Luke 15:24). This ought to encourage those who pray year after year for friends and family and the turning around of situations - to keep on trusting and praying.

When they *told him all the words of Joseph ... and he saw the wagons ... the spirit of their father Jacob revived.* He was then convinced, and said, *It is enough; Joseph is alive.* It is quite impossible to understand how Jacob felt; we can only imagine! But how did the brothers manage to convince him? Simply by telling him the truth! Notice verse 27: *But when they told him everything ...* (New International Version). No doubt they confessed their past lies and how they struggled to live with Joseph. But then they would go on to speak of Joseph's splendour and position - his majesty and authority. They would also speak of their reconciliation to Joseph, yes, and that he forgave them for everything. They were closer to Joseph than ever they had been. They would also share their excitement of what the future might hold.

Although Jacob was convinced and believed what his sons had shared, he still had to take a very traumatic decision, for two reasons.

Firstly, because he was over one hundred years old! At that age a great deal was being asked of him. This change would mean a new language, country, culture, friends and lifestyle. It would call for a complete uprooting of everything.

Secondly, many years before God had made Jacob a promise. *And God said to him, I am God Almighty: be fruitful and multiply. A nation and a company of nations shall come from you, and kings shall come from your own body* (Genesis 35:11). How would this square up with going to Egypt? This may have seemed to contradict his earlier promise, but not so. Jacob had that old Spirit-filled feeling - he knew that God was behind all this. Some time before this Jacob had exclaimed 'everything is against me', yet nothing was further from the truth - he just didn't know it at that time, it was all according to God's purpose.

The promise made to Jacob of nations and communities, including kings, coming from his own family lineage had not changed. God had planned blessing on a scale unimaginable through him, and what was now taking place was all part of it. What Jacob didn't know previously was that the birth of many nations would take place in Egypt, before moving back to Canaan some four hundred years later.

Even at such an advanced age Jacob is called to exercise faith. And how did God bring this about? He used Jacob's dearest possession, Joseph. God knew that it would take something special to uproot this man and his family. Never let us think for a moment that God's way is full of straight lines and obvious means. This story has more turns and twists than openly perceived. Yet the way for the believer is always 'by faith'.

During the years that Joseph had spent in Egypt, Jacob would not have had the slightest inclination regarding what God was doing. Those years may have seemed lean for Jacob of which the earlier period following Joseph's supposed death would have been spent in mourning. But God had not been idle, nor had his promise to Jacob been forgotten. The time was now right for all the strands to be pulled together.

God's great, wonderful and sovereign purpose is woven throughout this story in the smallest and most unexpected detail. God allowed things to happen that were sinful and wrong; he allowed injustice and pain that was seemingly undeserved, yet it was all for a purpose, bigger than all those involved could ever have understood at any given time.

The direction of the believer's life is in the hand of the Lord; he knows what is best for us in the long term. Had we to manage our own lives according to our own (limited) understanding, it would be quite disastrous. We are reminded in Proverbs 3:5-6 to trust in the Lord with all our heart and not to lean on our own understanding. It is when we acknowledge and submit to him, that he will direct our paths.

During our earthly journey God does not always give us special insight and wisdom, but he always invites our faith and trust, even through our darkest and most difficult times. Part of God's plan in Joseph's story involved the changing of people. Likewise, we too are called to a life of change and transformation if we are to experience God's very best. As we seek to follow our God, let us not stop believing when we cannot see clearly or understand all that is happening. Dr Sinclair Ferguson comments: 'There is no avoiding, and no substitute for, the sometimes long, arduous experience of discovering the will of God in our own lives. The will of God means death to our own will, and resurrection only when we have died to all our own plans.'

CHAPTER 16

Immigration and Reunion

Genesis 46:1-7, 26-34

So Israel took his journey with all that he had and came to Beersheba, and offered sacrifices to the God of his father Isaac. 2 And God spoke to Israel in visions of the night and said, "Jacob, Jacob." And he said, "Here am I." 3 Then he said, "I am God, the God of your father. Do not be afraid to go down to Egypt, for there I will make you into a great nation. 4 I myself will go down with you to Egypt, and I will also bring you up again, and Joseph's hand shall close your eyes."

5 Then Jacob set out from Beersheba. The sons of Israel carried Jacob their father, their little ones, and their wives, in the wagons that Pharaoh had sent to carry him. 6 They also took their livestock and their goods, which they had gained in the land of Canaan, and came into Egypt, Jacob and all his offspring with him, 7 his sons, and his sons' sons with him, his daughters, and his sons' daughters. All his offspring he brought with him into Egypt.

26 All the persons belonging to Jacob who came into Egypt, who were his own descendants, not including Jacob's sons' wives, were sixty-six persons in all. 27 And the sons of Joseph, who were born to him in Egypt, were two. All the persons of the house of Jacob who came into Egypt were seventy.

28 He had sent Judah ahead of him to Joseph to show the way before him in Goshen, and they came into the land of Goshen. 29 Then Joseph prepared his chariot and went up to meet Israel his father in Goshen. He presented himself to him and fell on his neck and wept on his neck a good while. 30 Israel said to Joseph, "Now let me die, since I have seen your face and know that you are still alive." 31 Joseph said to his brothers and to his father's household, "I will go up and tell Pharaoh and will say to him, 'My brothers and my father's household, who were in the land of Canaan, have come to me. 32 And the men are shepherds, for they have been keepers of livestock, and they have brought their flocks and their herds and all that they have.' 33 When Pharaoh calls you and says, 'What is your occupation?' 34 you shall say, 'Your servants have been keepers of livestock from our youth even until now, both we and our fathers,' in order that you may dwell in the land of Goshen, for every shepherd is an abomination to the Egyptians."

Last time we left the brothers sharing all the news about Joseph with their father. They arrived back with new wagons, supplies, money and the invitation to immigrate to Egypt. Without doubt, Jacob's joy and expectation would have been immense at the thought of seeing Joseph again; yet there were other issues which would have caused Jacob much soul-searching. Acting in obedience to the purpose of God will very often be tested; this would be the case for Jacob, as no doubt, he would ponder deeply over certain considerations.

- Jacob was being called to leave the land that God had chosen for him, which included the promise of future blessing beyond measure.
- Another consideration was his age - he was now 130 years old.

- The invitation to move to Egypt also presented a problem because Jacob was brought up to believe that Egypt was the most detestable place in the world.
- Jacob would have known that his grandfather, Abraham, got into trouble in Egypt. Furthermore, in Genesis 26:2 we are told that Isaac, Jacob's father, was instructed by the Lord 'not to go down to Egypt'.
- History and tradition were also against him moving to Egypt.

For these and possible other reasons Jacob must have been apprehensive and struggled from within, yet the thought of seeing Joseph again and also receiving the promise of future security would have been a tremendous pull. God knew that it would take something special to unearth Jacob from Canaan: Joseph was that someone special! However, Jacob was a 'man of God' and it would ultimately be his sense of divine direction that he would rest upon. Though pulled on every side, Jacob knew in his heart what was right to do; God was calling him to Egypt - and so, with mixed emotions of fear and joyous expectation, he decided to move, saying: *It is enough; Joseph my son is still alive. I will go and see him before I die* (45:28).

Just as God had a plan for Jacob and all his children, likewise, the Bible reminds us that Christians are people who have been called *according to the purpose of his will.* Indeed, as the apostle Paul writes in Ephesians 1:3-14 reminding believer's of their spiritual blessings in Christ, he says: ... *making known to us the mystery of his will, according to his purpose....* How wonderful it is to know that God has a plan for his children, and that he makes that plan known to them. Although this privilege is great and undeserved, we have, just like Jacob, the responsibility to live our lives being led by the Holy Spirit day by day; learning how to please God and sensitively obey him.

Sometimes when we face major issues or direction is needed, we may examine all the circumstances, use our common sense and seek the advice of mature Christian friends to help us understand what action to take. Yet, when all is said and done, we are called to live a life of faith and should only act in obedience when we hear the Lord speak to us. The prophet Isaiah in 30:2, writes, *And your ears shall hear a word behind you, saying, 'This is the way, walk in it'*. It was so with Jacob and ought to be so for all who follow the Lord.

After preparation, packing and many fond farewells, they set off for Egypt. They had not travelled very far when Jacob stopped at a place called 'Beersheba'. Why did he stop so soon? To worship God! He was giving God his rightful place; he was now back on track, listening to God and obeying him. This opportunity to offer worship to God was also a time for Jacob to rededicate himself to God. It was just like 'old times' again, for we read in verse 2: *And God spoke to Israel in visions of the night and said, 'Jacob, Jacob'. And he said, 'Here I am'.* Here we have intimacy and fellowship. Are these not the words the Lord wants to hear from all his children? It is said that 'God is not so much interested in our ability or inability - but rather, in our availability'. Little is much when placed in the Master's hands.

Following Jacob's worship and rededication, the Lord reassured him of the decision he had taken and the journey he was making to Egypt. *Do not be afraid to go down to Egypt, for there I will make you into a great nation.* For sure, Jacob's heart must have burned within him. Many years before he had wrestled with God; had been a dreamer and a schemer; now that old fire was aglow once more with a sense of God's presence and purpose. Jacob had been in a spiritual desert, now his spirit is revived and once more he moves out in faith. Moving to Egypt was very much part of God's great purpose, it wasn't a backward step - but a forward step of faith.

Notice how gracious and understanding God was with Jacob. In verse 4 God said, *I myself will go down with you to Egypt, and I will bring you up again, and Joseph's hand will close your eyes.* What amazing words indeed. Just as the Lord had been with Joseph, so now he promised to be with Jacob. The way ahead was new and uncertain, yet he would not be alone, the God of Abraham and Isaac his father was also his God, and he would never leave him or forsake him. This was a journey of faith; the only thing that Jacob could be certain of was God - and that was enough! How fitting are the words: 'I do not know what lies ahead, the way I cannot see, yet one stands near to be my guide - he'll show the way to me.'

Jacob had sent his son Judah ahead of this sizeable company (seventy in all) to make contact with Joseph. When he arrived, Joseph had his chariot prepared and headed off immediately to meet his father and family. All of Pharaoh's household would have known that Joseph's family were soon to arrive in Egypt and how excited Joseph was. Bearing in mind that Joseph's family were shepherds, and that such an occupation was an abomination to the Egyptians, Joseph would not cover up this fact. He was not ashamed of them. This is a lovely picture of Jesus, who is not ashamed of his family even with all their natural imperfection.

In Hebrews 2:12 we read: *That is why he is not ashamed to call them brothers, saying, 'I will tell of your name to my brothers; in the midst of the congregation I will sing your praise'.* This is exactly what Joseph would do as he presented his family unashamedly before Pharaoh.

We come to the moment when Jacob and Joseph come face to face. The last time Jacob saw Joseph was when he sent him off to find his brothers who were looking after their flock and report back on their situation (37:14). Little did Jacob know that it would be many years before he would set his eyes on Joseph again. In fact, the truth was, following the brother's lies to their father, allowing him to think that Joseph was dead, Jacob would never have expected to see Joseph again. From thinking Joseph to be dead, to meeting him as the governor of the land, provides us with a contrast that just cannot be imagined. Here is reunion; here is intimacy; here is glory and joy unspeakable.

The great hope and certainty for every believer is that one day we will see the Lord Jesus as he is; he who died for our sins and was raised in glorious power for our justification; he who is seated at the Father's right hand will present those he purchased with his own blood on the cross, before his Father in heaven.

We are told in verse 29 that Joseph *presented himself to Jacob, his father, and fell on his neck and wept ... a good while.* Words were not enough; tears would be the only appropriate language for such an occasion. Notice that Joseph 'presented himself' to his father. There was no swaggering or aloofness, no pride or self-exaltation, just humility and broken hearts being reunited. Two men coming together, more alive than ever they had been. This was no quick embrace; tears flowed for a while - 'a good while' we are told. Silence was golden as father and son tearfully hugged each other. Nothing on earth was more important to Jacob than this moment in time, described by him in this way: *Now let me die, since I have seen your face and know that you are still alive.*

Knowing, as previously mentioned, that shepherds were detestable to the Egyptians and that Joseph did not hide this fact; indeed he exercised great wisdom by making this known to Pharaoh immediately (*I will go up and tell Pharaoh*). He hid nothing and told his brothers to do exactly the same (verses 33-34). By going to Pharaoh on his brothers behalf Joseph was 'interceding and mediating'. Once again this reminds us of our Lord Jesus. Pharaoh responded by welcoming them and said, *The land of Egypt is before you. Settle your father and your brothers in the best of the land* (47:6).

The fact that they were shepherds would not be held against them because Joseph had acted on their behalf. Is this not a picture of our Lord Jesus acting on behalf of the sinner? We read in Hebrews 9:15,24: *For this reason Christ is the mediator of a new covenant, that those who are called may receive the promised eternal inheritance - now that he has died as a ransom to set them free ... Christ has entered ... into heaven itself, now to appear in the presence of God on our behalf* (New International Version).

And what of sinners who come to God just as they are, hiding nothing? Are they not saved by God's grace and welcomed into the wealth of God's Kingdom? Are they not *heirs of God and fellow heirs with Christ?* Do they not share in the wealth that belongs to Christ himself? To which we answer with an emphatic - yes! Only the best was to be good enough for Joseph's family. Likewise, only the best is reserved for those who have entered the Kingdom of God through faith.

CHAPTER 17

God meant it for good...total forgiveness

Genesis 50:15-26

15 When Joseph's brothers saw that their father was dead, they said, "It may be that Joseph will hate us and pay us back for all the evil that we did to him." 16 So they sent a message to Joseph, saying, "Your father gave this command before he died, 17 'Say to Joseph, Please forgive the transgression of your brothers and their sin, because they did evil to you.' And now, please forgive the transgression of the servants of the God of your father." Joseph wept when they spoke to him. 18 His brothers also came and fell down before him and said, "Behold, we are your servants." 19 But Joseph said to them, "Do not fear, for am I in the place of God? 20 As for you, you meant evil against me, but God meant it for good, to bring it about that many people should be kept alive, as they are today. 21 So do not fear; I will provide for you and your little ones." Thus he comforted them and spoke kindly to them.

22 So Joseph remained in Egypt, he and his father's house. Joseph lived 110 years. 23 And Joseph saw Ephraim's children of the third generation. The children also of Machir the son of Manasseh were counted as Joseph's own. 24 And Joseph said to his brothers, "I am about to die, but God will visit you and bring you up out of this land to the land

> *that he swore to Abraham, to Isaac, and to Jacob."*
> *25 Then Joseph made the sons of Israel swear,*
> *saying, "God will surely visit you, and you shall*
> *carry up my bones from here." 26 So Joseph died,*
> *being 110 years old. They embalmed him, and he*
> *was put in a coffin in Egypt.*

And so Joseph's family were welcomed by Pharaoh and settled in Egypt in a choice part of the land called Goshen. Before settling, Jacob had the privilege of blessing Pharaoh. This was only possible because God had been at work in Pharaoh's life; this would previously have been unthinkable. With the passing of time (about seventeen years) Jacob himself became ill. Before he died he requested that his sons present themselves to him, where he blessed them and at the same time defined their characters and prophesied their future. Chapter 49:28 records it this way: *This is what their father said to them as he blessed them, blessing each with the blessing suitable to him.*

Throughout the story of Joseph there are many lessons to learn and much to think about as the Spirit of God brings before us certain things for our consideration and help. Humility, suffering, patience, maturity, trust and the sovereign purpose of God are but a few. There is, however, one lesson that stands out: it is the need to understand the nature and meaning of 'total forgiveness'.

If we want to know why God exalted Joseph to the lofty position of Prime Minister of Egypt, it is because he learned in a spirit of humility to 'forgive and love' in a way that glorified God and blessed others. Forgiving and loving, even among God's people can often be very difficult. Yet through all of God's dealings with Joseph - all the seemingly horrid and unjustifiable experiences that no-one would wish upon themselves - God was able to produce in Joseph these two wonderful fruits.

We are not privy to all of Joseph's inner struggles or wrestlings with God, but we do know that God did not release him for exaltation and prominence until he was ready. We don't know at what precise moment in Joseph's heart that he was able to forgive his brothers, but until that time, Joseph was not ready and in bondage. Joseph had to forgive those who had mistreated and abused him without cause. And so God had to melt his proud heart. This took time, for the barrier of pride, can be a terrible stumbling block.

When the brothers came to Egypt Joseph made it clear to them that he 'totally forgave' them. He then proved it by providing for them for seventeen years. In spite of this, an unusual twist takes place. After Jacob had died the brothers came to Joseph desperately worried with a made up story. They suggested that their father, before he died, had left a message that Joseph should forgive them for all their transgressions against him. For seventeen years they had continued in some form of fear, not really accepting the forgiveness that Joseph had offered. Years before Joseph had said to them: *Come near to me, please ... And do not be distressed or angry with yourselves because you sold me here, for God sent me before you to preserve life* (45:4-5). Had his words meant nothing? They had not learned to receive his forgiveness!

In verse 17 we learn how Joseph responded to their rejection. We read: *Joseph wept when they spoke to him.* He was broken-hearted and deeply hurt. This was a gross insult. It meant that the brothers must have thought throughout all those years that Joseph had just been acting, being a hypocrite for the sake of his father. Nothing was further from the truth; God had transformed and sanctified Joseph. His life was a testimony to the grace and purpose of God. Joseph's rejection by his brothers reminds us of the words of our Lord as he thought on the unbelief of his own people: *How often I would have gathered your children together as a hen gathers her brood under her wings, and you would not* (Matthew 23:37).

There is a lesson here for all God's children. If we have truly accepted God's forgiveness through Christ's finished work on the cross; then it will be in evidence through our own transformed lives and the visible grace of God. Should we be unable to forgive others from the heart, then we have not yet learned to appreciate God's grace and forgiveness for ourselves.

As the brothers, and not for the first time, confessed their sin and sought Joseph's forgiveness, they fell down before him with a submissive spirit. *Behold, we are your servants,* they said. He did his best to reassure them, telling them not to be afraid, saying, *am I in the place of God?* He was not their Judge. What they had never grasped was the fact that throughout all that had happened, from those early days in Canaan, including Potiphar's house and prison, right up to the present time - God was working out his purpose. Joseph reminded them that although their former actions against him were intended for evil purposes, God allowed it for good! How remarkable it is that Joseph was able to say, *So do not fear; I will provide for you and your little ones." Thus he comforted them and spoke kindly to them.* Surely now the brothers would be at peace with themselves, Joseph and the Lord.

As in this story, so in our own lives, God is not only moulding and shaping us as individuals to be godly and resemble his Son the Lord Jesus: there will always be a greater and wider purpose in mind. From the cradle to the grave, through family, friends; work life and church life; through every aspect of life and living, there is a much wider picture. People whose lives we have touched, those who have been influenced by our lives and others who have influenced us. We will never understand this side of glory the full implications of our lives.

Throughout most of Joseph's life neither he nor his family could have been privy to the greater, sovereign purpose of God. What a blessing it is, that we can read this story from beginning to end and see what they could not at that time.

Verse 26, *So Joseph died, being 110 years old. They embalmed him, and he was put in a coffin in Egypt.* Here was a man of God who had many likenesses to our blessed Lord Jesus. In spite of dark and difficult times he kept the faith and experienced the continual presence of the Lord. How wonderful is the testimony of God's Word to Joseph: *And the Lord was with Joseph.* As he looked back and saw the hand of God upon all the circumstances of his life, he could say, *God meant it for good.*